INSTRUCTIVE OBJECT LESSONS

by

Joseph A. Schofield, Jr.

BAKER BOOK HOUSE
Grand Rapids, Michigan

ISBN: 0-8010-8002-9

Previously published as
53 Sunday Talks to Children

PHOTOLITHOPRINTED BY CUSHING - MALLOY, INC.
ANN ARBOR, MICHIGAN, UNITED STATES OF AMERICA
1974

Contents

I. *The Flower Clock* (New Year)　　13

II. *The Man Hanging on the Sign*　　16

III. *A Snowflake* (Winter)　　21

IV. *Tramped Down Snow* (Winter)　　24

V. *Fire* (Winter)　　28

VI. *The Greatest American* (Lincoln's Birthday)　　32

VII. *Your Heart* (Valentine's Day)　　36

VIII. *George Washington as Gouverneur Morris Saw Him* (Washington's Birthday)　　39

IX. *Venice*　　43

X. *The Communion Wine* (Communion)　　48

XI. *The Crying Stones* (Palm Sunday)　　51

XII. *The East Flower* (Easter)　　55

XIII. *What Our Mothers Give Us* (Mothers' Day)　　59

XIV. *Heroes* (Memorial Day)　　64

XV. *"Lions and Mosquitoes Do"*　　67

XVI. *Christ and Little Children* (Children's Day)　　70

XVII. *"Lift Ye Up a Banner"* (Flag Day)　　74

XVIII.	*One Red Rose* (Summer)	78
XIX.	*The Liberty Bell* (Independence Day)	81
XX.	*"A Mighty Man, But a Leper"*	85
XXI.	*Why Do We Celebrate Labor Day?* (Labor Day)	89
XXII.	*"Quit You Like Men, Be Strong"*	93
XXIII.	*A Great Discoverer* (Columbus Day)	96
XXIV.	*The Painted Tree* (Fall)	101
XXV.	*The Illuminated Waterfalls*	104
XXVI.	*The Broken Telephone Pole*	109
XXVII.	*Football* (Fall)	112
XXVII.	*A Real Letter About an Airplane Flight Across the Continent*	116
XXIX.	*Another Letter About the Flight*	119
XXX.	*Thanksgiving Is Giving Thanks* (Thanksgiving Day)	122
XXXI.	*The Baby and the Sunbeam*	125
XXXII.	*A Light Upon the Path* (Universal Bible Sunday)	128
XXXIII.	*The Mistletoe and the Orchid* (Sunday Before Christmas)	132
XXXIV.	*What Shall I Give?* (Christmas)	136
XXXV.	*The Worn Out Christmas Tree* (After Christmas)	140

CHAPTER I

The Flower Clock

(NEW YEAR)

❧☙

PHILIPPIANS 4: 8: " Finally, brethren, whatsoever things are true, whatsoever things are honest, whatsoever things are just, whatsoever things are pure, whatsoever things are lovely, whatsoever things are of good report; if there be any virtue, and if there be any praise, think on these things."

OBJECT: A small clock.

❧☙

"FINALLY, brethren, whatsoever things are true, whatsoever things are honest, whatsoever things are just, whatsoever things are pure, whatsoever things are lovely, whatsoever things are of good report; if there be any virtue and if there be any praise, think on these things." Here is the text for the boys and girls this morning, Philippians 4:8. And here is a familiar object —a small clock. It tells the time, doesn't it? You all know what it is for and you all either know already or are rapidly learning how to tell time, I am sure. I want to tell you this morning about a most wonderful clock I once saw.

When I was travelling in Europe some years ago, I

visited Switzerland. Switzerland is a wonderful country; filled, you know, with the most gorgeous mountain scenery; for this tiny, clean, lovely, little republic is located high up in the very heart of the Alps; those wonderful, snow-capped mountains in central Europe. We are told that probably more visitors come to Switzerland than any other country in the world.* And there is little wonder, for the country is so beautiful, so clean, so hospitable.

Among other places that I visited in Switzerland, I came to Interlaken. The name Interlaken means, as you can readily guess, the city between the lakes, for it is situated between Lake Brienz and Lake Thun. It is a beautiful little city, but I presume the thing that makes it most famous and the thing that brings most tourists to visit it, is the fact that it commands a wonderful view of the famous, snow-covered Jungfrau Mountain, one of the highest in all Switzerland. I went up that mountain on a wonderful railroad that runs up it part way on the outside and part way on the inside. But that is another story and I will tell you about it some day.

Now the center of the social and tourist life in the City of Interlaken is the Kursaal, a beautiful, big building for the entertainment of the guests of the city. Here concerts are given, games are played, lovely gardens are provided, cheery sun rooms with many comfortable chairs are laid out and magnificent fireworks are produced at night. And here at the Kursaal I saw a most wonderful thing, a Flower Clock, located in the grounds of the entertainment palace, in the beautiful flower

* "New Geography" by Wallace W. Atwood, p. 187. Copyright 1920 by Ginn and Company. Sincere thanks go to the publishers for permission to quote this and the next reference.

garden near the entrance. And I think this Flower Clock was the most wonderful clock I have ever seen.

It was laid out like a huge flower-bed. The face of the clock and all the figures were made of flowers, in their beautiful, bright colors; living, growing flowers. The hands of the clock were made of metal and moved over the flowers around the face of the clock telling accurate time. Little gnome figures under a canopy struck the hours on little toadstools! And every time any person told the time by looking at this clock, he saw beauty! Every time you wanted to know what time of day it was, you had to look at something beautiful, if you told time by the Flower Clock! Whenever you looked at the time, you saw something beautiful!

It was like a sun-dial I once saw. A sun-dial, you know, is an instrument that tells time by the shadow of the sun cast upon a plate by an arm that is attached to the plate. Perhaps you all have seen a sun-dial. The Romans and the Greeks had them 2000 years ago. Isaiah tells us that King Ahaz had one in Jerusalem 750 years before that. And the Egyptians had something like sun-dials, a form of a shadow clock, 3400 years ago.* Well, the sun-dial that I saw had inscribed on it a sentence that ran something like this: " I count none but sunny hours." You cannot tell time by a sun-dial unless the sun is shining to make the shadow on it. And so the one I saw told all who looked at it that it counted only the bright and sunny hours. Only the bright and beautiful hours counted!

Now that is good advice. Count only the bright and beautiful hours. That is good advice for the New Year

* " Ancient Times " by James Henry Breasted, p. 91. Copyright 1916 by him. Published by Ginn and Company.

upon which we are just now entering. In the New Year ahead of us, note the beautiful things. Ignore or forget the unpleasant ones. May every day of the New Year be like the Flower Clock—every passing minute a thing of beauty; or like the sun-dial—counting only the sunny hours.

So Paul speaks to us and gives us advice in the Bible. That is what our text really means that I read to you at the beginning. " Finally, brethren, whatsoever things are true, whatsoever things are honest, whatsoever things are just, whatsoever things are pure, whatsoever things are lovely, whatsoever things are of good report; if there be any virtue, and if there be any praise, think on these things." Think on the things that are true and honest and just and pure and lovely and of good report and of virtue and of praise. Look for these things in the New Year. Find them. And forget the other things; the things that are bad and mean and cruel and wicked and evil. Think on the things that are fine and lovely and beautiful. Think on these things!

CHAPTER II

The Man Hanging on the Sign *

❧

REVELATION 15: 1: " And I saw another sign in heaven, great and marvelous."

OBJECTS: For this sermon I gave each child present a picture post-card of the great Wrigley sign described in it. These

* Facts and figures about the sign were furnished by the Wrigley Company and are used by permission.

cards were furnished me by the Wrigley Company. If these post-cards are not available, any picture showing an electric sign would do very well.

⁓ ♡ ⁓

Our text this morning, boys and girls, is found in the last book in the Bible, the Book of Revelation; in the 15th chapter and a part of the 1st verse: " And I saw another sign in heaven, great and marvelous." This text tells about a wonderful sign in heaven. The picture on the cards that the ushers have given you is a picture of a sign on earth. I want to tell you something about this sign whose picture you have.

I was in New York City not long ago on some church business. And in the evening I was walking in Times Square, the busy center of the night-life of that great city. I was walking along Broadway, between 44th and 45th Streets, and I saw, across the great open space of the square, a most wonderful electric sign. It was, I think, the most wonderful electric sign I ever saw. It was Wrigley's Spearmint Gum sign. Many, many people stopped to look at it and the sidewalk across the square from the sign was lined with interested spectators.

This wonderful sign reached across one whole city block, from 44th Street to 45th Street. It was built on top of a two-story building and was itself ten stories high. It cost a million dollars to build it. In the center was a giant figure of a green " Spearman " in a blue circle, sitting on a package of Wrigley's Spearmint Gum bigger than a box car. He moved his arms and pointed his fingers to messages about Wrigley's Spearmint that constantly changed at the top and the bottom of the sign. Around him were 11 huge tropical fish—

the largest 42 feet long—all in brilliant colors. These fish appeared to be swimming amid waves of sea-green light. The waves of the sea and the fins of the fish moved. Their scales flickered. Huge white bubbles rose from the fishes' mouths. The effect of brightly-colored fish in a moving sea, live fish in a real ocean, was beautiful and wonderful indeed.

This electric sign was the largest sign of its kind in the whole world. It contained 1,084 feet of Neon tubing; almost 70 miles of insulated wire; 29,508 electric lamps. It gave as much light as five United States Lighthouses combined. And the electric current required to light it would illuminate a city of 10,000.*

That evening when I looked at it, I noticed that a great crowd on the sidewalk across the street was deeply interested in something about it, something moving on it. And as I looked more closely, I discovered that there was a man hanging on that sign, moving about in front of it. And all the people were watching him. He was hanging on a mechanism of ropes and pulleys by which he could swing himself up and down and across the entire face of the sign. Twelve stories above the street, he would swing himself now up and now down and then clear across the entire face of the sign. I watched him and wondered what he was doing. And the more closely I watched the more readily I discovered what his business was 'way up there, hanging on that electric sign. He was replacing the burned-out bulbs. He had two bags swung from his shoulders. One of them probably contained the new light bulbs and the other no doubt contained the

* This sign was dismantled in the spring of 1942 to save electric current and steel for war production.

burned-out lamps. It was a very interesting sight to
see this man, in his dangerous occupation, swing up and
down and across that wonderful electric sign to keep it
brilliant by replacing burned-out bulbs with new ones.

I

Now as I looked at that sign, I knew it was the
largest and greatest electric sign in the whole world.
Yet there is a sign more important. Our text tells us
that. And the sign that is more important is not an
electric sign at all. Here is what our text says: "And
I saw another sign in heaven, great and marvelous."
There is a sign in heaven that is more important than
this sign on earth. The heavenly sign is great and marvelous. I am speaking now of the star in heaven when
Christ came into the world. That was another sign.
That was a great and marvelous sign. It told the whole
world that the Saviour had come, that Christ was born.
That was a greater sign and that was more important
news than any sign on earth or any advertising news
that man can see.

II

Now in the second place, this sign I saw in New
York City made all Broadway brilliant with light. Yet
there is a light more important, much more important,
much more wonderful than any electric light that
makes the great thoroughfare of Broadway as light as
day. The more important light is the Light of the
World. This greater light, this more important light,
you know, is Jesus Christ. He said Himself, you know,
" I am the Light of the World."

III

The man who was working on that sign that night was very small compared to the sign itself. How small he looked against its bright face! How like a tiny spider he seemed climbing and crawling and swinging himself in front of that wonderful display of light and color and movement! The sign was a whole block long. He was only a man. The sign was ten stories high. He was only an ordinary man. How small he was compared to it! Yet the sign could not run properly without him. It took a man—no doubt several men—to make the sign run correctly and do its work. The man was small, the sign was great. But the great sign just would not run without the man. He was working to keep the sign going. Yet there is a work in the world more important. And the work that is more important is a work you and I can do. We may be small, weak and little and humble and not important. Yet God wants us to work for Him. God wants us to help keep His light shining in the world. Just as the man on the sign helped keep the sign's light shining in the night, so we are to help God keep His light shining in the world. For you remember Christ also said, " Ye are the Light of the World." Our work is to shine for Him; to help keep His light shining.

IV

Of course boys and girls enjoy Wrigley's Spearmint. You do, don't you? Yet there is an enjoyment that is more important. It is the joy of being a Christian. I think boys and girls ought to enjoy the pleasures of life; candy and chewing-gum and ice-cream and games and fun. That is all fine. But just remember that there is an enjoyment even more wonderful and even more important. That is the enjoyment of being a Christian. There is no greater joy. There is no greater fun.

CHAPTER III

A Snowflake *

(WINTER)

JOB 38: 22: "Hast thou entered into the treasures of the snow?"

ISAIAH 1: 18: "Come now, and let us reason together, saith the Lord: though your sins be as scarlet, they shall be as white as snow."

OBJECTS: Some pictures of snow crystals photographed through a microscope. Such photographs, or drawings made from them, frequently appear in newspapers and magazines or can be found in an encyclopædia.

G OD asks a question, boys and girls, about the snow. "Hast thou entered into the treasures of the snow?" This question that God asks is found in His Word, in the Book of Job, chapter 38, verse 22. God asked it first of Job. But I think He asks it now of us, especially at this time of the year when the snow

* Much of the material used in this sermon came from an article written by the Rev. E. J. Pace, D.D., in the *Sunday School Times* of March 19, 1932. Both author and publishers have graciously given permission for use of the material here and the author of this volume expresses his indebtedness and his gratitude.

is so beautiful all around us outdoors. " Hast thou entered into the treasures of the snow? "

We love the snow, don't we? There is nothing I like better than a great, blustering snowstorm, so beautiful, so grand, so majestic. And I am sure that all of you feel the same way about it. The snow is great to play in, both when it comes tumbling down out of the sky and when it lies on the ground or is piled up in some great heap somewhere. It is great fun to run in it, to slide on it, to build forts out of it, to make snow men and snowballs. We boys and girls just love the snow. But this morning I want you to think of just one snowflake. For just one single snowflake is made up, you know, of many, many tiny little crystals of ice that stick together and make a flake of snow.

Now thousands of these tiny ice crystals, so small that you cannot really see them at all with the naked eye (you can see the snowflake but not the many tiny crystals that combine to make it) have been photographed by Mr. Wilson A. Bentley of Jericho, Vt. For over thirty-three years and up to the time of his death, this grand, old man used to take snowflakes and put them under the microscope and take pictures of the crystals that made up the flakes. And in all this time, over a third of a century, he said he never found two crystals that were exactly alike. They were always very beautiful, when viewed through the microscope or in the photographs that were taken through the microscope, almost always symmetrical and almost always having six sides or six points. Many of them looked like glorious six-pointed stars. Some took a design that looked like six pairs of frogs' legs kicking out from the center. Some looked like kewpie heads, six in a circle, one like grandfather's clock, with the hours marked off in six pairs; one like a gorgeous lace doily. One had the design of a horseshoe within it; one was shaped like a bobbin; another looked for all the world like six drooping petals of an iris blossom; some were like birds; some like bats. But in all their beauty and in all their variety, no two were ever found to be exactly alike. Here are some drawings of some of Mr. Bentley's photographs of snow crystals. See how interesting and how beautiful they are.

Certainly such beauty in nature must have been made by a Great Artist. Such rare beauty in such tiny crystals that only the microscope can discover must have been put there by the greatest Artist of the Universe, God Himself. And this same great Artist must be also the Great Architect, for these crystals are formed so perfectly. They are so complete, so symmetrical, so well balanced, that their great plan must be the product of God alone. The lovely falling snow, the beautiful white expanse of the snow on the countryside, the lovely clinging of the wet snow on trees and bushes always make me think of God, the Maker of beauty. But even more do we think of God when we understand the beauty and the wonder in each of the millions and billions of crystals that fall every time it snows.

Just think of it! How many millions of billions of flakes of snow fall on one acre of ground in one hour of a snowstorm. And each flake made up of many tiny crystals. And not one crystal like any other that has fallen in the same or in any other storm. What a great Artist and what a great Architect God must be! What a wonderful Maker the snow has; and you and

I! If God can do that, make every falling crystal of snow different from every other one that is or ever has been, is there anything that He cannot do? Our God who makes the snow can do anything!

Now one thing more. The snow speaks to us not only of God's greatness but also of His love. The snow speaks to us of grace. For the beautiful, white, fluffy snow falls on the dirty earth and covers up the black and dirt with a lovely mantle of pure white. Here is a picture of God's grace to mankind. For just as the pure, white snow covers up the dirty, black earth; so God cleanses our sins and forgives us for them, if we have faith in Him and come to Him in trust. And God Himself has told us that the snow is a picture of His forgiveness and His love. For in Isaiah 1:18 we read His own promise: " Come now, and let us reason together, saith the Lord: though your sins be as scarlet, they shall be as white as snow."

CHAPTER IV

Tramped Down Snow

(WINTER)

PSALM 122: 1: " I was glad when they said unto me, Let us go into the house of the Lord."

OBJECT: A snow-shovel.

THERE is a very familiar text in God's Word that I think many of you boys and girls know. It is found in Psalm 122, verse 1. If you do not know it already I know you will all want to learn it as soon as you can. This is the way it goes: " I was glad when they said unto me, Let us go into the house of the Lord." This is our text this morning.

A few days ago I was shovelling the stone walk in front of the manse after one of the heaviest falls of snow of the winter. In our North Country we get some rather cold weather. And sometimes we get a heavy fall of snow. On that day there was a lot of it on the main walk that runs in front of our house. And before I got to the job, many people had walked along that sidewalk. It was easy to shovel the snow off the walk, however, in the places where nobody had stepped. You know how people walk along the street soon after a snowstorm. One person comes along and makes the track. The next person steps where he had stepped. And the next and the next, until there is quite a beaten path down through the center of the walk. When people pass each other on the sidewalk, they have to break out a new path. But there are usually places where nobody has stepped at all. Now these places were easy to shovel. The snow was light. It had not been stepped on. It was easily removed.

Where only one or two persons had walked, to pass other people walking along in the beaten path, the shovelling was still easy. The snow was packed down a little bit, but not too tightly; and it was easy to shovel it off. Yet even in these places, I could not get every drop of snow off the walk; because the heavy tramping of the feet that had stepped on it ground some of it down so tightly that it stuck to the stones beneath. But most of it was easy to clean off.

But whenever I tried to shovel the place where many

people had walked on the snow, that was a different story altogether! Here the shovelling was hard, for here the snow had been packed down tight and solid. Many feet had tramped over it. It was very hard to clear away. In fact some of it, that which was packed down the hardest, simply could not be cleared away at all. Some of the tramped down snow had to be left on the walk. All I could do was to shovel away the top layer or two and leave much of it sticking fast to the stone walk.

And as I shovelled that sidewalk, some of it easy to clean, some of it a little harder, and some of it very hard to shovel, I thought that this was the way with habit. That snow on the sidewalk, some of it light and fluffy, some of it packed a little together by a few feet, some of it packed down tight by many feet, was very much like habit. There are two kinds of habits, you know, some bad and some good. And that snow on that sidewalk that morning made me think of both.

I

Some of our habits are bad. Now a bad habit is easy to break if we never start it. (That's the snow that was not tramped on at all—easy to remove.) You will never need to worry about breaking a bad habit if you do not start it. (I did not worry about removing the snow where nobody had walked.) Remember that. Don't start bad habits; and there are many of them. Don't begin them! Don't lie. Don't be mean. Don't be selfish. Don't be disagreeable. Never steal. Never cheat. Never swear. Don't start smoking dirty cigarettes. Don't ever touch liquor. Never start these habits and you will never have to worry over stopping them.

And if you have started any bad habit, one of these or some other, stop it at once. For it is not impossible to break a habit if you have only committed it a few times. (This is the snow that was only walked on by a few feet.) If you have made the mistake of starting a bad habit, stop it now before you do it too many times. (I got the snow pretty well off where only a few feet had trod.)

But when a bad habit has become firmly established by our doing it over and over, when we have practiced a bad habit many times, it is almost impossible to break it; it is almost impossible to stop. (That's the snow that was tramped down by many feet and that could not be removed.) That's the way with habit. Don't let a bad habit get so firmly established that you cannot break it. (I couldn't get the tramped down snow off the walk.)

II

And fortunately it is the same way with good habits. And you know many of these, too. I hope you know them well and will know more and more of them. There is cheerfulness—that is a good habit. Then there are honesty, helpfulness, and many others. There is going to Sunday School. That is a good habit, a very good habit. And so is going to church.

Like bad habits, good habits will not start unless we begin them! The way to get a good habit going is to begin. There is no other way.

And like bad habits, good habits can be broken, too, if we have practiced them only a few times. So if we do not want to break a good habit; if we want a good habit to develop and become a part of us, we must *keep at it.* Begin it. That's the way to start it. Keep at it. That's the way to make it grow.

And like bad habits, again, good habits are very hard to break once they are really established, once they have really become a part of us. So keep at your good habits—being cheerful, being honest, being helpful, going to Sunday School, going to church. Keep at them. Keep them up. Make them part of yourselves. Get them firmly established. Then they will be hard to break, almost impossible!

Church-going is a habit, as I have just said, a good habit, one of the best! Get this habit. Keep it up. Develop it. Make it part of yourselves! Then you will know what the Psalmist meant when he said, in our text, " I was glad when they said unto me, Let us go into the house of the Lord."

CHAPTER V

Fire

(WINNER)

JAMES 3: 5: ". . . the tongue is a little member, and boasteth great things. Behold, how great a matter a little fire kindleth! "

PROVERBS 26: 20: "Where no wood is, there the fire goeth out."

OBJECT: A piece of wood or a small fireplace log.

I WANT to speak to the boys and girls this morning about Fire. And to begin with, I want to read them a text from God's Word. It is found in the Epistle of

James, the 3rd chapter and the 5th verse: ". . . the tongue is a little member, and boasteth great things. Behold, how great a matter a little fire kindleth." In this text James is talking about the tongue. He compares it to a fire and tells us that a little fire can kindle a great blaze.

The other evening I was sitting in front of the fireplace in the manse. We had had a fire there but the logs were all burned down and there was nothing left in the fireplace but some small, dying coals. The room was still a little chilly and I thought it would be a good idea if I kindled another fire. So I took some shingles that I was using then for kindling wood and placed some of them on the coals of the old fire that was almost out. Above the pieces of shingles I put two or three logs. And in a very few moments there sprang up in that fireplace a fine blaze. The dying embers had caught the shingles. The shingles had caught the logs. And in a few moments I had a splendid, blazing fire. The fire caught from the embers only. There was no blaze there before. But if the conditions are just right, you can get a blaze from embers only. A little fire, a fire almost gone, you see, can produce a great blaze. Isn't that interesting?

Now that is just what James said in our text. He said that a little fire can kindle a great matter! And he also said that, exactly so, a little wrong word can do great harm. " The tongue is a little member, and boasteth great things. Behold, how great a matter a little fire kindleth! " The tongue can speak one little word, sometimes; and if that one little word is a bad word, a wrong word, a harmful word, a mean word, how much damage can be done! You know that is true. You know how some wrong word of yours does great harm sometimes. That is what James meant.

And, just so, a good word will often do great good. Don't forget that. Sometimes a good word, spoken in the right place, will make somebody very happy, will do somebody great good. As one little wrong word can do much harm, so one little right word can do much good.

But now there is another side of this matter of fire. And for this other side of the picture I want to read you another text. This time it is from the Book of Proverbs, the 26th chapter and the 20th verse: " Where no wood is, there the fire goeth out." I have just told you that sometimes you can make a big fire from a very little fire if you put wood on it and if you put it on in just the right manner. Now I want to tell you the other side of the thing; that if you do not put the wood on, the fire goes out!

Suppose you are building a fire, either in a fireplace or out in the open on a hike, and you put some large logs on it over your kindling wood. To make those big logs burn, you soon discover that you must have them touch each other. One log alone will not very often catch fire from the kindling wood. The kindling will blaze up but the log will not catch and soon the kindling is all burned up and the fire is out. To catch your logs, you must have more than one and there must be a contact. Your logs must touch.

Now that is usually true of a fire. And do you know what it makes me think of? It makes me think of our contact with Christ. We must touch Him if we are going to blaze for the truth. We must be in contact with Him if we are to catch the fire and the light that

He came into the world to give to the world. If we are going to shine for Jesus, if we are going to blaze for the truth, if we are going to be on fire for the Gospel, we must keep in constant contact with Jesus Himself; we must be in touch with Him. We must catch our enthusiasm for the Truth, our light for the Gospel, our fire for the Kingdom of God from Him.

That is why many people are not on fire for Jesus. They are not in touch with Him. Remember He is the Source of life and light and we must get our life and our light for Him. And we cannot get them from Him unless we are in touch with Him. Our hands must be in His hand. Our life must be in contact with His life. We must catch our enthusiasm and our light and our fire from Him.

And so fire teaches us two things this morning. A little fire kindles a great matter. A little word, whether good or bad, can cause great good or do great harm. For logs to catch on a fire, they must touch each other. For us to catch the fire of the Gospel, we must be in touch with Christ. Maybe we can think of these two things whenever we see a fire blazing on the hearth!

CHAPTER VI

The Greatest American

(LINCOLN'S BIRTHDAY)

෨෨෨

2 SAMUEL 5: 10: " And David went on, and grew great, and the Lord God of hosts was with him."

OBJECT: A picture of Abraham Lincoln.

෨෨෨

How many of the boys and girls know whose birthday is tomorrow? That's right, put up your hands. Now, another question. How many of you know whose picture this is that is displayed this morning in the church? Fine. I'm glad so many know. And it is the same person, isn't it, whose birthday is tomorrow and whose picture is here in church today—Abraham Lincoln?

I am going to tell you a true story this morning. One day when I was visiting in Washington, D. C., the wonderful city that is the capital of our country, the United States of America, I went to see the beautiful Lincoln Memorial. It is a perfectly lovely building, with great and gorgeous columns around it; and all of it reflecting into a perfectly marvelous lagoon or pool, at the end of which the building is situated. In the main room of the building, at the center of it, stands a huge monument; which is a representation of Abraham Lincoln seated upon a chair. The statue is a very wonderful statue, perfectly made, carved out of marble. It is a tremendous thing, much bigger than any real man, but made so big and impressive so that people can the better see it and enjoy looking at it. It is really a giant-sized statue. Well, while I was standing in front of this great, marble statue, there came up to it, to look at it, a small boy and his mother. They stood near me admiring the wonderful figure of Lincoln seated upon the chair. I had never seen either the mother or the boy before but I could not help hearing what they said. For the little boy looked up into the face of his mother and remarked:

" Mother, was Lincoln really that big? "

I

Abraham Lincoln was a big man. In several ways he was a big man, one of the greatest of all men. First of all, he was a big man, physically. Of course, when he was living he was not so big as this lovely statue of him is. This statue is called a " colossal " statue because it is so huge. It is much, much larger, to be sure, than Abraham Lincoln was in real life. But just the same Lincoln was a big man. He was big in frame and big in strength. He was broad-shouldered and possessed great muscle and great strong arms. He was a very tall man, six feet, four inches in height. He was called " the rail-splitter " because of his prowess in splitting logs up into fence rails with the axe. He was a big man and a strong man.

II

In the second place, Abraham Lincoln had a big mind. He was a very smart man. He was one of the very best of lawyers. He went to Congress, you know, and showed what a fine mind he had while there. He be-

came President of the United States and was one of the
wisest and one of the finest of all the Presidents we
have ever had. His mind was big and great and fine
and brilliant. The language he used was beautiful and
pure. His famous Gettysburg Address was one of the
very greatest speeches ever spoken in the English language and it will never die out of the memory and the
heart of mankind. He had a big mind.

III

And then he had a big heart. He longed all through
his life to help the slaves. When he was a young man
he saw something of the cruel treatment that many of
these poor, ignorant, abused black men had to un-
dergo. You know when Lincoln was young, colored
people in this country were still slaves. Men and
women and boys and girls were owned and bought and
sold, body and soul, just like cows or pigs. And very
often their owners did not treat them well at all—
beating them, abusing them, and sometimes allowing
them to die. Lincoln loved these simple, humble, trust-
ing people, so unfortunate and so unhappy, and he
longed with all his heart to help them. But he loved all
people, the white as well as the black, his enemies as
well as his friends, the south as well as the north.
When he became President this great country of ours
was split apart in a dreadful and a bloody Civil War.
Lincoln was determined to win that war because he
loved his country and determined that it must be preserved whole. But he did not hate the south. He loved
those who were fighting him and his cause. And after
he was reelected and was inaugurated President for the
second term, in his great speech which is called his

Second Inaugural Address, he used these wonderful words: " With malice toward none; with charity for all."

IV

In the fourth place, Lincoln did a big job. He saved this great country of ours from going to pieces. It was split in two by the war. He bound it together once more and prevented its ever falling apart again. That is what we call saving the Union. He saved the nation and kept it one united nation. And that is why we still have one nation today instead of forty-eight little, separate ones. And besides saving the country, he was able, at last, to free every one of the slaves in this country. Never again were the negroes held in bondage in America. Every one of them was freed by this great man who did such a big job.

V

And finally, in the fifth place, he made for himself a big name. He made himself into one of the greatest and biggest and finest men who ever lived on this earth; our greatest President; the greatest American. That, after all, is the name he earned for himself and that is what most people call him today, " The Greatest American." Isn't that a big name?

So Lincoln was a big man, was he not? He was big physically; he had a big mind; he had a big heart; he did a big job; he made for himself a big name!

In the Bible, in the 2nd Book of Samuel, the fifth chapter and the tenth verse we read: " And David went on, and grew great, and the Lord God of hosts was with him." This, our text today, tells us that David, the greatest King of Israel, grew great and the Lord was with him. That is what made him great. God was with him. Now I think today we can apply this text about David, the greatest King of Israel, to Abraham Lincoln, the Greatest American. For I am sure we can say the same thing about him. " And Lincoln went on, and grew great, and the Lord God of hosts was with him." Lincoln was great, became the Greatest American. And it certainly was true that the Lord God was with him. That is what made him great. God was with him. And if we do God's will, if we seek to please God, if we try to do what God wants us to do, then one day it may be said of us that we grew great and that the Lord God of hosts was with us!

CHAPTER VII

Your Heart

(VALENTINE'S DAY)

PROVERBS 4: 23: " Keep thy heart with all diligence; for out of it are the issues of life."

OBJECT: A heart cut out of pasteboard or colored paper.

I HOLD in my hand, boys and girls, an object very familiar to you all at this time of year, a paper heart. How many of them we see on Valentine's Day. How many we receive and how many we send to our friends! With this heart in my hand, I want to read you our text for today. It is found in the Book of Proverbs, the 4th chapter and the 23rd verse: "Keep thy heart with all diligence; for out of it are the issues of life."

The heart, you know, is a symbol of love. The heart stands for love. That is why we use it on Valentine's Day. You send a paper heart to your mother on Valentine's Day to tell her you love her. A young man who loves a young woman and intends some day to marry her, may send her a colored heart on Valentine's Day to show his love for her. We send colored hearts or heart-shaped boxes of candy or bright valentines of some other nature with hearts prominently displayed on them to our friends on Valentine's Day to show our friends that we love them. The heart stands for love and that is what makes it the proper symbol for Valentine's Day.

But the heart is also a symbol of your life. The heart stands for life as well as for love. We often speak of our hearts when we mean our lives. That is what our text means, you see. "Keep thy heart with all diligence; for out of it are the issues of life." Let us put that in our own modern language. "Keep your heart very carefully; for out of your heart come the things that make your life." Your heart makes your life.

In another place, in this same Book of Proverbs, the inspired writer tells us the same thing in another way. For in Chapter 23, verse 7, this is what we read: ". . . as he thinketh in his heart, so is he." That means that as a man thinks inside of him, that is the kind of a man he is. What is in a man's heart decides what kind of a man that man really and truly is.

Your heart determines your life. That is what it means. What kind of a person you are inside, that is

the kind of a person you are going to be outside. What
kind of a person you are in your heart, that is the kind
of a person you are going to be in your acts. What you
are inside you, in your heart, will determine the kind
of things that you are going to do. If you have a good
heart, you will have a good life. If you have inside you
a bad heart, then your life will be bad. If your heart is
pure, your life will be pure. Now that is very simple,
isn't it? That is very clear. That is easy to understand.

So you see how important it is to keep your heart
pure, good, kind and loving. For out of a pure heart
there will come pure thoughts. Out of a good heart
there will come good words. Out of a kind heart there
will come kind acts. Out of a loving heart there will
come loving deeds. "Keep thy heart with all diligence;
for out of it are the issues of life." That is what Solomon said in our text from the Book of the Proverbs.
"Keep your heart very carefully," we would say, "for
out of your heart come the things that make your life."

But how can you keep your heart very carefully?
Give it to Jesus. That is the way to keep your heart. Indeed the only way to keep your heart is to give it away
—to Jesus Christ. He will take care of it. He will make
it and He will keep it pure and good and kind and loving. The only real way to be sure that you are going to
keep your heart with all diligence is to make sure that
Jesus will keep it for you. Give it to Him and He will
guard it and keep it. To keep your heart you must give
it away—to Him.

The Bible tells us that, too. In different language,
but with exactly the same meaning, the Bible tells us
that the way to keep your heart with all diligence, very
carefully, is to give it to Jesus. In the Book of Joshua in

the 24th chapter and the 23rd verse we find these words: ". . . incline your heart unto the Lord God of Israel." " Incline your heart " means to give your heart. And so this verse tells us to give our hearts to the Lord and He will keep them. The way to keep your heart is to give it to Jesus.

CHAPTER VIII

George Washington as Gouverneur Morris Saw Him *
(WASHINGTON'S BIRTHDAY)

෬◦◦◦

PROVERBS 9: 10: " The fear of the Lord is the beginning of wisdom."

OBJECT: A picture of George Washington.

෬◦◦◦

'THE fear of the Lord is the beginning of wisdom." That, boys and girls, is our text this morning, taken from God's Word in the Book of Proverbs, the 9th chapter and the 10th verse.

How many of you know whose birthday is next Thursday? Hands up! That's fine! His picture is on the pulpit this morning, isn't it? George Washington's birthday comes this week. That is why we have the

---

* The quotations in this chapter are taken from " Honor to George Washington," an official publication of The United States George Washington Bicentennial Commission, to whom cordial thanks are given for permission to reprint them here.

flags in church this morning and his picture hanging on the pulpit. We remember his birthday because George Washington was the Father of our Country.

Now there was another man who lived at the same time as George Washington, though he was a little younger and so lived a little longer. He thought a very great deal of Washington and said some very wonderful things about him. His name was Gouverneur Morris. And Gouverneur Morris, like George Washington, was a very great man during the important period when our great country was just being formed. With many other great men, these two had much to do with getting America started and making it a strong and a great country. During the hard and trying period of our War for Independence and during that other hard time that came after that, the establishment of the Constitution of our country, Gouverneur Morris and George Washington did great and wonderful work.

Morris was a member of the Continental Congress, that great, representative lawmaking body that united the thirteen colonies before they became independent of Great Britain. He was really the father of our system of coinage. Other men later on worked it out, but Morris really gave them the idea. He was a member of the Constitutional Convention that framed that wonderful document we call the Constitution of the United States. He helped write that important document. Indeed he gave much of the actual wording to it. At one time he was Ambassador, or Minister as they called it then, to France. Later he was a member of the United States Senate. So you see that Gouverneur Morris, too, was a great man.

Our town was named after him, as you all know so

well. That is why we are particularly interested in Morris and in all that he did or said.

When Washington, the Father of our Country, died in 1799, Gouverneur Morris, who had known him so well and who had loved him so much, paid him a great tribute. His praise of George Washington was very high indeed.

I

Among other things, he said that George Washington was dignified. These are the very words that Morris used: " So dignified his deportment, no man could approach him but with respect—none was great in his presence." Washington was noble, tall, handsome, dignified. And I think we can be dignified, too, boys and girls. Let us imitate Washington in this. Let us not be silly, foolish, thoughtless. Let us be dignified.

II

Next, Gouverneur Morris said that George Washington was high thinking. This is the way he said it: " His judgment was always clear, because his mind was pure." Washington thought of high things, noble things, pure things. He had a clear mind, a pure mind, a high-thinking mind. He did not think mean, low, miserable thoughts. He thought of high and noble things. And so should we, boys and girls. Our minds should be clear and pure. Our thoughts should be high and noble. Let us, like Washington, be high-minded and high thinking.

III

Then the third thing that Morris said about Washington was that he was brave. And this is the way he said that: " In him [that is, in Washington] were the courage of a soldier, the intrepidity of a chief, the fortitude of a hero." That means, you see, that Morris said that George Washington was a brave soldier. And we know he was, for he won a long, hard war, the American War for Independence. Then he called him a fearless chief. And we know that was true because he was the head of the army; and then he was the head of the nation, the first President of the United States. And Morris said he was a courageous hero. And that was true, also. The country loved him. He was their leader. He became our National Hero. Certainly, Washington was brave. And we, too, boys and girls, can be brave.

IV

And the fourth thing Gouverneur Morris said about Washington was that he was wise. Listen to his words: " Knowing how to appreciate the world, its gifts and glories, he was truly wise. Wise also in selecting the objects of his pursuit. And wise in adopting just means to compass honorable ends." That is to say, Washington knew what to work for, the independence of this country, a strong nation to be built up out of the thirteen colonies. And he knew how to get it by honest and by right means. He was wise because he knew what to work for and what to fight for. He was wise because he knew how to get what was right and proper by using right and proper means. But we, too, can be wise, boys and girls. And we, too, should be wise.

But what made George Washington so great, what gave him all these grand and noble qualities about which Gouverneur Morris spoke? I think I know the answer. I think I can explain to you why George Washington was so great. He believed in God. He was what we call a churchman. He believed in and feared God. He went to church and he was an officer in the church. He was a Christian. And I am convinced that it was God who helped him to be dignified, to be high thinking, to be brave and to be wise. You remember what our text says, do you not? " The fear of the Lord is the beginning of wisdom." God made George Washington great because God helped him to be dignified, high thinking, brave and wise. And in the same way God will make us great, if we will but let Him. I do not mean that we all can become President of the United States. God does not want us all to be Presidents. But God does want us all to be great and good. And God will help us if we let Him.

CHAPTER IX

Venice

2 KINGS 2: 11: " And it came to pass, as they still went on, and talked, that, behold, there appeared a chariot of fire, and horses of fire, and parted them both asunder; and Elijah went up by a whirlwind into heaven."

REVELATION 21: 21, 23: " And the twelve gates were twelve pearls; every several gate was of one pearl: and the street of the city was pure gold, as it were transparent glass. . . . And the city had no need of the sun, neither of the moon, to shine in it: for the glory of God did lighten it, and the Lamb is the light thereof."

OBJECT: A picture of Venice.

༺⚬ঌ

WOULDN'T every one of you boys and girls like to go to Venice some day—Venice, that beauty-spot of Italy; the world's most unique city and the city which most visitors call the world's most beautiful city? I am sure you would and I hope you all may be able to do so some day; for I am sure you would never forget it and it would be a precious memory as long as you live.

When I first arrived in Venice and came out of the railroad station I looked about for a taxi to take me to my hotel. But there was no taxi there. Instead there was a boat! For there, in front of the railroad station, was no street at all but a stream of water! There was a great stone platform or plaza that led from the portals of the station to the edge of the water, but there were no automobiles to be seen, no horses, no street-cars. Just a canal and some boats. And so we had to get into a little boat, called a gondola, and this carried us to the door of our hotel, which also had its front door not on a street but on a canal!

I

And that is the way people get about the city of Venice from place to place. They go in boats on hundreds of little canals that wind in between 120 little islands upon which the wonderful city is built. People can go all over the city, of course, but the regular way to go is in boats. I was told that there are only five

horses in the entire city of Venice. And four of these
are bronze horses that stand over the main entrance to
the famous cathedral of San Marco or St. Mark's. And
the fifth is another bronze horse upon which the bronze
statue of a famous Venetian general sits. There are no
automobiles in the city, either. For where could they
use them? There are no streets, as we understand
streets. The canals that wind between the many islands
are the streets and the vehicles are boats. There are no
streets at all that are made for horses and automobiles.
There are walks that run across the various islands and
wind in and out between the buildings and there are
many bridges that connect the islands all together. So
a person could walk all about the city, across the different islands, across the bridges from island to island.
But he cannot ride about the city unless he rides in a
boat on a canal.

Now it may seem very strange to us for people to go
about a city on canals instead of on streets. But there
are many different ways that people get from place to
place in this old world of ours. I remember very well
seeing a picture of Tibet, or some other place in central
Asia. This picture showed a swiftly flowing river and
people were crossing the stream by means of a wire
cable strung across above it and they crossed it in little
baskets hung from that cable and pulled across the
stream. I remember my visit to Amalfi, another beauty-
spot in Italy, and the hotel 'way up on the mountain-
side where we lived while there. There were 199 steps
that wound in a long procession up the mountain-side
to that hotel. And many people were carried up those
steps in a sort of a basket-chair to get to the hotel.
There are various ways to go about, you see.

And thus God can take us to heaven when our time comes and He is ready to receive us. We cannot understand at first how people travel on canals instead of streets in Venice. So we may not understand just exactly how God manages to take us to His wonderful home in heaven. But He does. And even if we do not understand it, we must know that He can do it. He did it for Elijah, you remember, in a very wonderful way. 2 Kings 2: 11 tells us: " And it came to pass, as they still went on, and talked, that, behold, there appeared a chariot of fire, and horses of fire, and parted them both asunder; and Elijah went up by a whirlwind into heaven." God does not take us in that wonderful way but He can take us to heaven just the same.

II

Another thing about Venice that impressed me was the fact that there are both dirt and beauty there. The narrow streets or alleys, the little walks that people use across the islands, are usually very dirty, with papers and refuse thrown carelessly about. So are the canals dirty, with garbage and other refuse floating in them and lizards crawling out of them and up the sides of the houses. When the tide goes out, I suppose this dirt goes out with it to the sea. But part of the time the canals are quite dirty. Yet Venice is a city of great beauty too. When you look down you see the dirt. When you look up and out you see the beauty ·—magnificent bridges arching across the canals, ancient houses and palaces built along the water's edge, wonderful churches built on the various islands. A city of great charm and great beauty. And you can look above the dirt and see the beauty. That is what we should do in life. Look above the dirt and see the beauty! Look for the beauty in all of life. If you look for it, you can always find it!

III

The third thing I want to tell you about Venice is something of the magnificent beauty of the sunset over the city and the glory of the night on the Grand Canal. We saw the sunset over the city of Venice from an island a little distance away, called Lido. Coming back from that island, across the lagoon, we beheld the most glorious sunset I had ever seen. Below was the city, purple and dark in the twilight. Above it was the color of the sunset, red and gold, like a patch of glory in the sky, brilliant and magnificent. Still above that was the dark sky, overcast and black. The most wondrous sight I can remember.

Night on the Grand Canal and on the lagoon beyond the famous Piazza of St. Mark is beautiful, too. As you ride in your little, black gondola along the canals you are delighted to see the flickering lights of houses and palaces reflected out across the water. And when you come to the great lagoon, you find hundreds of other gondolas there, lovely lights everywhere, beautiful music floating out across the water from large, flat barges anchored out in the lagoon on which sit players and singers. A beauty-spot indeed. A place of loveliness and splendor. The earth is lovely. We live in a wonderful world. But heaven is even more lovely and more wonderful. Listen to the way God's Word describes it in the Book of Revelation, the 21st chapter and the 21st and 23rd verses: " And the twelve gates were twelve pearls; every several gate was of one pearl: and the street of the city was pure gold, as it were transparent glass. . . . And the city had no need of the sun, neither of the moon, to shine in it: for the glory of God did lighten it, and the Lamb is the light thereof."

CHAPTER X

The Communion Wine

(COMMUNION)

❧❧❧

JOHN 10: 10: " I am come that they might have life, and that they might have it more abundantly."

OBJECTS: A bottle of colored liquid plainly labelled " POISON " and either a bottle of grape juice or a cup of Communion wine.

❧❧❧

I HAVE a text for the boys and girls this Communion Sunday. It is found in the Bible in the Gospel of John, the tenth chapter and the tenth verse: " I am come that they might have life, and that they might have it more abundantly." These are words that Jesus spoke. He said that He had come into the world that we might have life.

Now it is necessary for us to eat and drink if we are going to live, if we would keep going the life that God gives us. Both food and drink are needed to sustain life. Now one form of drink that is commonly used is the juice of the grape, pressed out of the fruit that grows on the vine and carefully prepared and bottled so that it will keep and be ready for use whenever it is needed. It was this juice of the grape that Jesus used for the drink when He gave His disciples that wonderful memorial meal that we call "The Last Supper." And it is this same juice of the grape that we use when we have Communion. Members of the church will soon be drinking it. For as we drink it we show that we accept Christ as our Saviour and as our Lord.

I have brought with me this morning two vessels containing liquid. One is this bottle of bright-colored liquid which you can see from the label is poison. The other is this little glass cup containing some of the Communion wine that the members of the church are so soon to drink to show that they accept Christ. Now this liquid that I have told you is poison will, if it should be drunk, bring death. If any one should drink this bottle of poison, he would die. But this cup of Communion wine is just the opposite. Because to drink this means life. This poison produces death. This Communion wine produces life.

More than that, this Communion wine shows us that it is Christ who gives us life. Every time we drink it we remind ourselves and show the world that we believe that Christ gives us life. And not ordinary life merely, but eternal life, the life that will know no end, the life that will never be ended by death. And as the church members shortly will drink this wine, they will be showing to all who are willing to see that Christ gives life to men; the eternal life that will have no end.

Now that is what our text means. Jesus says to us: "I am come that they might have life, and that they might have it more abundantly." Jesus came into the world that we might have life. That means that Jesus gives us life.

But how can Christ give life to us? What authority and what power has He to give life to those who are His, those who believe on Him, those who accept Him as their Saviour? Why, He can give life to us because He took death for us! It was for us that He went to the cross and died. It was for us that He suffered there and gave His life. It was for us He took the sins of the world on His shoulders and bore them to the cross. It was for us He died so that He might give life to us. He took our death that He might give us His life.

Let this bottle of poison stand for death. Let this Communion wine stand for life. Jesus gave us this (the Communion wine) because He took for us this (the poison). He gave to us life, because He took for us death. Now of course He didn't drink poison. I do not mean that. But He did drink the cup of death. He did drink death. He was nailed to a cross. And He went to it voluntarily. He let His enemies hang Him there. He went to His death willingly and gladly because His death gave us life. And that is why and that is how He can give life to us, who believe in Him, today. And that is just what He meant in our text. He came to the earth to give us life and He gives us life by Himself dying in our place and in our stead.

And that is the meaning of the Communion. We shall take it soon to show that through Christ's death, we have life. When we drink this wine we are showing our faith in that truth. So when you see the church members in a moment drink this Communion wine, you can remember that they are doing it to show that Christ has given them life.

CHAPTER XI

The Crying Stones

(PALM SUNDAY)

❧❧❧

LUKE 19: 40: "And he answered and said unto them, I tell you that, if these should hold their peace, the stones would immediately cry out."

MATTHEW 21: 15–16: "And when the chief priests and scribes saw the wonderful things that he did, and the children crying in the temple, and saying, Hosanna to the son of David; they were sore displeased, And said unto him, Hearest thou what these say? And Jesus saith unto them, Yea; have ye never read, Out of the mouth of babes and sucklings thou hast perfected praise?"

OBJECT: A cobblestone.

❧❧❧

ON the first Palm Sunday, when Jesus came riding into Jerusalem upon the back of the little donkey and proclaimed Himself King, great crowds gathered about Him and shouted His praises. They waved branches of the palm-trees in the air and cast them at His feet as a carpet. That is why we call this day Palm Sunday. They also cast their garments in the street under the advancing feet of the little beast upon which the Coming King rode. And all along the line of march they shouted His praises; they called Him King; they sang songs of joy; they offered thanks to God. And some of the Pharisees from among the multitudes came to Jesus and asked Him to rebuke His friends and

make them stop singing thanksgiving to God and calling Jesus King and praising Him. " And he answered
and said unto them, I tell you that, if these should hold
their peace, the stones would immediately cry out."
Jesus meant by that exactly what He said. That if the
people should stop praising Him, the stones would at
once cry out and praise Him instead. Yes, stones. The
stones would start to talk and would praise the Lord if
the people stopped doing so—stones like this one I
have in my hand, cobblestones of the street, stones
along the road, stones in the hillsides, stones in the
walls of the houses. If people did not praise Christ, the
stones would.

And on the next day, the day after the first Palm
Sunday, when Jesus came into Jerusalem once again,
the children kept up the praising in the Temple, singing songs of happiness and thanksgiving and calling
words of love and loyalty and adoration and worship
to Jesus their King. This time the chief priests and
scribes complained and told Jesus to make the children
stop. " And when the chief priests and scribes saw the
wonderful things that he did, and the children crying
in the temple, and saying, Hosanna to the son of
David; they were sore displeased, And said unto him,
Hearest thou what these say? And Jesus saith unto
them, Yea; have ye never read, Out of the mouth of
babes and sucklings thou hast perfected praise?" Jesus
asked them if they had never read in the Bible that
even little babies can praise God.

I

Now what Jesus said to the Pharisees on Palm Sunday and what He said to the chief priests and scribes

on the day after Palm Sunday show to us that He is to
be worshipped. Jesus is to be worshipped. He wanted
worship. He received it when the people gave it to
Him. He invited it. He asked for it. He expected people to worship Him. He is our Teacher. The greatest,
finest lessons come from Him. He is our Saviour. He
saves us from our sins. He is our Master. He gives us
orders and we are to obey them. He is our Lord. He
owns us and we are His. But even more than that, He
is our God. Once He said, you remember, " He that
hath seen me, hath seen the Father." And again He
said, " I and my Father are One." He is God, one with
the Father and to be worshipped with the Father. He
never stopped people when they worshipped Him. He
expected and wanted it.

II

More than that, we see from these events that He
wants children to worship Him. He expects men and
women to worship Him. But He also wants children
to do so. You remember how He took little children in
His arms, and put His hands upon them and blessed
them. You remember how He once said, " Suffer the
little children to come unto me, and forbid them not:
for of such is the Kingdom of God." Children have a
place in the Church and children ought to be in that
place. Children ought to be taught to worship Christ.
Christianity is for men and for women. But it is also
for children. Christ wants the children. He wants them
to worship Him.

III

In the third place, we see from these events how true

it is that the whole creation declares His praises. The whole world, everything that God has made, praises Christ, His Son. Look about you and see how all nature praises Christ. Now I do not mean that all creation, that is all nature, praises Christ today in exactly the same way those stones in Jerusalem would have done if the people had kept quiet. Jesus said that if the people had kept quiet, the stones would actually, really and truly, have spoken out with tongues. They really would have said actual words. God would have made them really talk. Of course God did not have to do that that day, because the people did not keep silent but did cry out in praising Christ. But God would have done it if the people had kept silent. So it is not like that, not with real tongues and actual words that nature praises Christ today. But nature praises Him really just the same. It is a beautiful world, isn't it, in which we live? And all the beauty of the world praises Christ who made it. The stones He has made praise Him— how beautiful some of them are, how grand, how majestic. The trees, also, that He has made praise Him. The lovely streams of flowing water. The vast and towering mountains. The gorgeous sunset. The magnificent evening sky. All creation declares the praises of Christ.

IV

Then, why should not men and children? If the sky and the earth and the water in the sea; if all creation and all things that God has made, praise Christ; why should we not do so? We have tongues and we have words. If rocks and trees and streams and mountains can praise Christ, surely men and women and little children who have hearts to love Him and voices to sing His praises, and words in which to express their devotion, can and should always praise Him and adore Him and worship Him.

Let us praise Christ as our King.

CHAPTER XII

The Easter Flower

(EASTER)

∽◦◦∾

1 JOHN 3: 14: ". . . from death unto life, . . ."

OBJECT: A Japanese paper flower which is folded tightly together but which opens when placed in a glass of water. Often these Japanese paper novelties can be obtained in the form of a plant or shrub apparently growing in a tiny imitation flower pot. If these are unobtainable, a flower without the pot will do.

∽◦◦∾

O N this beautiful Easter morning, I have a beautiful Easter text for the boys and girls. It is found in the Word of God, in the First Epistle of John, the third chapter and the fourteenth verse, in the middle of the verse: ". . . from death unto life, . . ." I truly hope that all of you will get out your Bibles when you get home and look up this verse. For it is a splendid Easter verse. ". . . from death unto life, . . ."

I have here in my hand a little Japanese paper flower. You see it is an imitation plant or shrub growing in a tiny, imitation flower pot. But it is all folded up and dried out. It is not a thing of beauty because it looks dead. It looks for all the world just like a little cluster of folded paper stuck in a tiny, imitation flower pot. It looks dead and useless and ugly. But I drop it into this glass of water and ask you to watch it closely. Behold, as the water gets into its folds and begins to loosen up the tightness of the little bundle, a wonderful thing happens. Gradually the flower unfolds itself. Gradually the flower opens up. Gradually the flower comes to life! Now what was an ugly bundle of tightly folded paper has turned itself into a beautiful flower with all its color and all its brightness shining through this glass of water. The flower is now alive and beautiful and glorious. It has come from death unto life.

But this flower in this glass of water in my hand is only paper. It is not a real flower. But what it has just done, coming from death unto life, is a picture of what the real flowers of springtime do every year. The gorgeous flowers that we so eagerly look for in the spring have all apparently died the fall before. I am sure you all have noticed how the lovely flowers, every one, droop, lose their petals, dry up, topple over and die with the coming of the fall. They are gone. They are dead. But when spring comes again and the warm, spring rain falls upon them, they burst forth once more. Like the water in this glass, the rain gives new life to the flowers. New shoots start up. New stalks push themselves through the ground. And at last new blossoms burst forth in all their beauty and in all their glory. What was dead in the fall is alive again in the spring. Of course only the bodies of the flowers died the fall before. The real life of the flowers was bound up in the bulbs or roots under the ground or in the seeds that the flowers dropped. But the thing I want you to notice is that what seemed to die in the autumn was alive again in the spring. That is what makes spring so beautiful. Millions and millions of glorious flowers that were apparently dead come back to life and beautify the world.

Now the beautiful flowers of spring make us think of Easter. They are what we call a symbol of Easter. Because they remind us of the fact that Christ died. And they remind us further of the other fact that Christ came to life again! But here is the difference. The flower only seems to die. Its life is preserved for it in the bulb or root or in the seed. Christ, our Lord, really did die on the cross. He died there for our sins. He died for us, in our place, for our sins. And His death was a real death. He was really dead. But on Easter morning, the first Easter that ever was, He rose again from the dead and became alive! And so the flowers of Easter that seem to die and then seem to come to life again are beautiful pictures of Jesus Christ who really did die for us and then really did come to life once more. Flowers are only pictures or symbols of Easter. Christ's death and resurrection give the true meaning to Easter. Christ really came from death unto life. Christ was dead. He came to life again. He is alive for evermore!

But, boys and girls, there is one more thing that the Easter flower reminds us of. It tells us that just as Christ died and rose again, so we, some day, unless He returns to the earth beforehand, shall die; and then, too, some day, we shall rise. Some day, if Christ does not come back to the earth beforehand, our bodies shall die. But our souls will live on. That is what death is for us. Our bodies die. They are put in the ground. But our souls live on in heaven where God is. We do not die for our sins. Christ did that for us. Death for us is just the leaving of our bodies behind while our souls go to dwell in heaven with God. But then, some day, our bodies will come back to life, when our souls return from heaven and come back into our risen bodies. Just as Christ's body came back to life, so, some day, our bodies will come back to life. They will be new and glorious, made like unto His own glorious body, but they will be our true bodies, our own bodies, come back to life.

Now that is the promise of Easter. That is the picture the Easter flower brings to us. That is what makes Easter so happy. Christ is alive! We, too, shall live!

CHAPTER XIII

What Our Mothers Give Us

(MOTHERS' DAY)

꼬◡ꊁ

1 SAMUEL 1: 27–28: " For this child I prayed; and the Lord
hath given me my petition which I asked of him: Therefore also I have lent him to the Lord; as long as he liveth he shall be lent to the Lord. And he worshipped the
Lord there."

OBJECT: A carnation.

꼬◡ꊁ

TODAY is Mothers' Day. Here is a carnation. A carnation, you know, is the flower of Mothers' Day.
We all try to wear a carnation (or some other flower)
on Mothers' Day in honor of our own mothers. White
carnations are worn in memory of the mothers who
are dead. Colored carnations are used to honor those
mothers who are still living.

Benjamin West, one of the greatest artists of America, once said, " My mother's kiss made me a painter."
And Abraham Lincoln, America's greatest statesman
and her noblest President, said, " All that I am or hope
to be, I owe to my angel mother." Here, then, are two
great men who praised their mothers for what they
had done for them. And we might speak of many,
many more who have paid tributes to their mothers for
what their mothers had given them. For it is always
so. Our mothers give much to us, and we should be
grateful.

I want to speak to you this morning about four different men in the Bible and tell you what their mothers gave to them. I want to mention four of the greatest men of history and show you that each one of them received much of his greatness from his mother.

First, then, take Moses, the mighty Lawgiver, the Founder of the Hebrew Nation, one of the greatest men of all time. Moses was a mighty man of faith, and it was his faith that made him so great. But the thing I want to tell you this morning is that it was his mother who gave him his faith. When he was a tiny baby, you remember, and the Egyptians were trying to kill all boy babies who were born into the families of the Hebrews, Moses' mother put her tiny child into a little basket or ark and placed him tenderly on the surface of the mighty River Nile. The Princess found him, you remember, and saved his life and adopted him as her own child and took him to the palace. But she needed a nurse, you know, and hired his own mother to take care of him. So it was Moses' own mother who really brought him up and who taught him his religion, his faith in God. And later, when Moses had become a man, he delivered Israel out of the terrible bondage of Egypt, gave to the people the wonderful Law, organized them into a mighty nation. His faith made Moses great, and he received his faith from his mother.

Next, consider Samson, the strong man, one of the strongest men of history. It was his mighty strength that made him famous, was it not? And it was his mother who gave him his strength. She dedicated him to God, you remember, before he was born, and the vow was that no razor was ever to come on his head and no wine or strong drink was ever to enter his mouth. And just as long as Samson through his life kept this vow, his strength was tremendous and he could do mighty things. And so, when he was grown up, his mighty strength showed itself. Once he killed a lion with his bare hands, tearing him to pieces. Once he carried off the gates of a great city wall. One time he broke great cords that bound him. And throughout his life he destroyed many enemies of his country. His strength made him famous, and his mother gave him his strength.

And now we come to Samuel, a man of courage. I really think that it was Samuel's courage, more than anything else, that made him one of the greatest men of all time. And his courage his mother gave to him. You remember how when God answered her prayer and gave her a son, she lent that son to the Lord. That is our text, 1 Samuel 1: 27–28. She brought her young child to the Tabernacle and left him there in charge of the High Priest, saying, " For this child I prayed; and the Lord hath given me my petition which I asked of him: Therefore also I have lent him to the Lord; as long as he liveth he shall be lent to the Lord. And he worshipped the Lord there." That took courage, to leave that little child in the Tabernacle among strangers, in care of the priests. And it gave courage to Samuel. His mother left him there to be brought up in God's House and to become God's servant, and every year, we read, she came to see him and brought him a little coat. And when Samuel was grown, he stood out bravely against the wicked sons of Eli, the High Priest. He led Israel against the wicked enemies, the Philistines, and defeated them. He anointed the first King of Israel, Saul, and later on, when Saul had failed and had disobeyed God, he bravely went to him and told him that God had rejected him as King. And then Samuel anointed, for God, the young David as the next King. Great courage marked all of Samuel's life. And it was his mother who gave it to him.

For our fourth man, let us take John the Baptist. His mother gave to him his love for Christ, and John the Baptist's love for Christ, more than anything else, made him one of the world's greatest men. John's mother was Elisabeth, a cousin of Mary, Jesus' mother. That made John and Jesus cousins, too. Elisabeth loved Christ with all her heart, and she believed that He was her Lord and Master. She told Mary so, and she taught John so. She loved Jesus Christ so much that she made her young son, John the Baptist, love Him, too. And later on, when John grew up, he showed his great love for Christ. For he told his own disciples or followers to leave him and follow Christ. He pointed Christ out as the Lamb of God that taketh away the sins of the world and tried to get every one to love Jesus as he loved Him. His love for Christ marked his whole life, and he received that love from his mother.

But these same things our mothers give to us. They give us faith as Moses' mother gave him faith. They give us faith because they teach us about Christ. They teach us to pray. They teach us to talk to God. They help our childish lips form our first prayer,

> " Now I lay me down to sleep;
> I pray Thee, Lord, my soul to keep."

Our mothers today give us strength, just as Samson's mother gave him strength. They look after our health.

They see to it that we have good food to eat. They give us milk to drink. They provide warm and clean clothes for us to wear. They keep us from catching colds, from getting sick. They give us strength.

Our mothers today also give us courage, just as Samuel's mother gave him courage. They teach us to be brave in pain and in trouble. Our mothers help us in times of distress and danger. Men's courage, almost always you will find, comes from their mothers.

And our mothers today, also, give to us our love for Christ, just as John the Baptist's mother gave him his love for Christ. They teach us to love Jesus who first loved us. They teach us to know Him, to adore Him, to worship Him. It is usually our mothers who tell us how much Jesus Christ did for us and how much He is doing for us all the time. It is usually our mothers who give to us children our love for Christ.

CHAPTER XIV

Heroes

(MEMORIAL DAY)

❧ ☙

2 SAMUEL 1: 27: "How are the mighty fallen, and the
weapons of war perished!"

❧ ☙

THE boys and girls have a beautiful text this morning. It is found in God's Word, in the Second
Book of Samuel, the first chapter and the 27th verse:
"How are the mighty fallen, and the weapons of war
perished!"

Jonathan had been killed in battle. And David, his
friend, mourned him. David loved Jonathan very much
indeed, and Jonathan loved David. The story of the
love of these two young men for each other is one of
the most beautiful stories in the entire Bible. And
when David learned that his dear friend, Jonathan,
was dead, he honored him in a song. How highly he
praised him. How truly he showed his love for Jonathan in the fine things that he said about him. And the
lamentation that he made, the song that he sang for
Jonathan, ended with the words of our text: "How
are the mighty fallen, and the weapons of war
perished!"

Memorial Day will be celebrated next Friday. On
that day we honor the soldiers and sailors who died
for their country. It is a wonderful day, then, you see,
because it is a day of memory; a day of honor; a day

of tribute. The nation mourns and honors those who died for it.

Some little time ago we all read of a most terrible accident that happened to a new submarine of the United States, the SQUALUS, which sank into the sea and failed to rise again in a test dive near the Isle of Shoals, off the coast of New England, at Portsmouth, New Hampshire (May 23, 1939). The under-water boat did not rise again as it should from its dive into the water. The crew, the men who run the boat, were in it. It was a terrible accident and everybody on shore, when they learned of it, felt sure that every man in that boat would die. But something was done that was never done before in submarine history. Thirty-three men were rescued from that sunken ship, 240 feet deep in the sea, after thirty hours in the dark, cold submarine. The rescue was a wonderful feat, accomplished by the use of a kind of diving bell—a huge, hollow, metal ball—let down over the submarine. It was then attached to one of the ship's hatches, permitting the men who were still living to crawl up into it, a few at a time, and then to be hauled up out of the water to the surface.

Thirty-three men were saved. But twenty-six men lost their lives, for they were in a part of the boat that had been flooded. And it was the flooding of part of the vessel that caused the submarine to fail to rise in the first place and caused the twenty-six men in that part of it to drown. Twenty-six men lost their lives in that accident. Twenty-six men gave their lives to their country, for they were sailors working on one of Uncle Sam's ships of defense, one of America's naval vessels. Really and truly these men died for their country. They did not die in war. They did not fall in battle. For our nation was at peace with all the world. But just the same they died for their country. They gave their lives just as truly for America. And so I think the words that David used for Jonathan can be used for them, " How are the mighty fallen! "; and the words he used for the laying down of Jonathan's sword and spear can be applied to the sunken vessel, " And the weapons of war perished! " These men were heroes. They died for their country. They gave their lives for America.

But the lesson of Memorial Day for us, boys and girls, and the lesson of the deaths of these twenty-six men for us is simply that we, too, can serve our country. We don't need to be killed in battle to serve our country. We don't need to die in a submarine to serve the America we love. We can serve our country by living a Christian life. We can serve our country by helping make the United States a Christian country. And by living a Christian life, by helping make America a Christian country, we shall be serving our nation in the most important way of all. If we want America to be great, we must make America truly Christian. When the lives of all Americans are Christian lives, then America will be truly a Christian country and a great country indeed.

We all can be heroes, just as really and truly as those twenty-six men who gave their lives for their country in the sunken submarine. We all can be heroes. Some day we might have to die for our country, even as they died for their country. But if we never have to die for our country, and I truly hope we never shall, we certainly can live for it. And we can be just as real heroes living for our country as dying for it. Live for

America. Help make it Christian. Help make it
truly great.

CHAPTER XV

" Lions and Mosquitoes Do " *

❧

SONG OF SOLOMON 2: 15: "Take us the foxes, the little
foxes, that spoil the vines: for our vines have tender
grapes."

OBJECT: A picture of a lion.

❧

H ow many of you boys and girls know what a lion
is? Put up your hands. Isn't that a silly question,
for you all know? How many of you ever saw a real,
live lion? Hands up! Fine; I see many of you have
been to the circus or the zoo. I do not really need to
show you this picture, then, do I? For you know very
well what a lion is. Now here is another question,
another silly question. How many of you know what a
mosquito is? How many of you have ever seen one, or
heard one sing in your ear as he came buzzing around
your bed at night? How many of you have ever been
bitten by one? I think you all know what I am talking
about, all right.

*   *   *   *   *

Well, I have a true story for you this morning, and
I think a true story is the best kind of a story, don't

---

* I want to express my deepest gratitude to my wife, Mary Lewis
Schofield, for her innumerable helps in preparing this volume, especially for suggestions back of Chapters XXIII, XXXVII and LIII.

you? One day a little boy I know—I shall not name him—remarked, " Lions bite." I presume that he had been looking at a picture book or maybe had been coloring and came across a picture of a great, fierce lion. And he remembered the zoo he had visited or the circus he had attended and recalled the King of Beasts, examples of which he had seen, and remembered how fierce and cruel he could be. And so he said, " Lions bite." Then he turned to his father and asked a question.

" Do frogs? "

" No," his father said, " frogs do not bite."

" Do mice? "

" No," his father replied again, " as a rule mice do not bite people. Mice are afraid of people, dreadfully afraid, and they scamper away whenever they hear or see people coming. And so mice almost never bite people."

" But mosquitoes do? " the little boy asked.

" Yes," the father answered, " mosquitoes do."

" Lions and mosquitoes do," the little boy returned. Now he had the information he wanted. " Lions and mosquitoes do. Lions and mosquitoes both bite."

* * * * *

And that, boys and girls, is just exactly the way it is with sin. Big sins and little sins—both bite! Sins like lions that can devour you and one day kill you; and sins like mosquitoes, that can probably only prick your skin; both bite. Lion sins and mosquito sins. Big sins and little sins. Both bite.

Little lies, the kind we sometimes call white lies, are still lies; and they bite and hurt, ourselves and others.

Little lies may not be so bad as big lies, but they are still lies; they are still sins; they are still wrong. And they hurt; they do harm. They bite.

A little stealing, like a piece of candy from brother or sister, or a cookie from the pantry shelf without mother's permission, is still stealing and it is wrong and sinful. And it harms other people and also, worst of all, ourselves. It is sin, and it bites. And while a little stealing may not be so bad as a big stealing, it is still stealing; it is still sin; and it bites!

There is a very interesting text in the Book of God which fits in right here. It is found in the Song of Solomon, the 2nd chapter and the 15th verse. "Take us the foxes, the little foxes, that spoil the vines: for our vines have tender grapes." Here were some foxes that were doing great damage to the grapevines. They were only little foxes, just tiny, little, cute fellows; but they were spoiling the beautiful grapevines and the lovely grapes were tender. And these little foxes were doing just as much damage as great, big foxes. Indeed much more in this case. Because the big foxes were not touching the vines. They were off somewhere doing some other damage. And it was the little foxes who were spoiling the vines. And the fact that they were little did not excuse them one bit. They were only little animals, but they were doing great damage. They were destroying the grape crop. Little sins can be just as wicked, can do just as much damage, sometimes, as big sins.

Indeed, it has been well said: " Little sins are the parents of the greatest." * Do not forget that. " Little

* Jamieson, Fausset and Brown: " A Commentary, Critical and Explanatory, on the Old and New Testaments."

sins are the parents of the greatest." Beware the little sins that grow into big ones! Beware the little foxes that spoil the vines! Little sins and big sins are both sins! Little sins and big sins both bite! Lions and mosquitoes do!

CHAPTER XVI

Christ and Little Children

(CHILDREN'S DAY)

❧ ♡ ❧

MATTHEW 19: 14: " Jesus said, Suffer little children, and forbid them not, to come unto me: for of such is the kingdom of heaven."

❧ ♡ ❧

THE children have a text this morning, a children's text. You all must know it, I am sure. But if you do not, you will want to learn it. It is found in God's Book, in the Gospel according to Matthew, the 19th chapter and the 14th verse. It is one of the most beautiful texts and one of the most tender in the whole Bible. " Jesus said, Suffer little children, and forbid them not, to come unto me: for of such is the kingdom of heaven."

Today is Children's Day. We always have a Children's Day, once a year, in church. And it is right that we should. For Christ has always meant much to children; in His own day, down through the ages and today. And children in turn should love Him.

I

To begin with, Christ was once a little Child, Himself. And that is a wonderful thought, isn't it? Jesus Christ, the wonderful Teacher, the glorious Healer, the powerful Miracle-Worker, the loving Saviour, the majestic King of Kings and all-powerful Lord of Lords, was once a little Child. Just like you, He was born a baby, and grew up as a little Child. He experienced childhood, just as you and I have experienced it. There was one great difference, of course, as the Bible explains to us. He was without sin, and you and I are not. But in all other respects, His childhood was similar to ours. He grew up as a little Boy in a simple, humble home. He was once a Child and He therefore knows all about our childhood. He can sympathize with us; can feel with us; can understand us. And He also hallowed childhood—that is, made it glorious and beautiful and divine.

II

In the second place, Christ loved little children. When He grew to be a Man and walked about the regions of Galilee and Judæa, we are told over and over how much He loved the children. The Bible tells us in one place that "He laid his hands on them" (Mt. 19: 15). In another place it says that He "took them up in his arms" (Mk. 10: 16). And again it says "and blessed them" (Mk. 10: 16). He loved little children when He was here on this earth. He loves little children still. Surely children in return ought to love Him!

III

In the third place, He told us Himself that the Kingdom of Heaven is like little children. This should draw children to Jesus, shouldn't it? For He used children as an illustration or as a picture to show people what heaven was like. The Kingdom of Heaven, He said, is like little children. Now He said that in our text, didn't He? " Jesus said, Suffer little children, and forbid them not, to come unto me: for of such is the kingdom of heaven." The Kingdom of Heaven is like that. The Kingdom of Heaven is made up of people like children. What are the things that make childhood so beautiful, that make children so lovable? Are they not such things as faith and trust and forgiveness? A child has faith. A child trusts. A child forgives and forgets. Well, such things make up the Kingdom of Heaven, Jesus said. The very things that make children children are the very things that make the Kingdom into Heaven. And just because heaven itself is made up of faith and trust and forgiveness and all the sweetness and innocence and beauty that belong to little children, for that very reason, children should know that Jesus belongs to them and they to Jesus.

IV

And finally, in the fourth place, we want to remember always that Christianity, the religion that Jesus gave to us, changed altogether and forever the place of children in the world. Before Christ came, people used to ignore children, pay no attention to them. They used to mistreat them, be cruel and heartless to them. Or they used to exploit them, that is, make them work and toil for their elders and then take the money that they earned away from them. Children were misused, abused, mistreated. But Christ changed all that. Because He took little children into His arms and placed

His loving hands upon their heads and blessed them, He made people love children and take care of them and help them and look out for them and make them happy instead of miserable and forlorn and sad. Never forget, boys and girls, as long as you live, that Christ did for children what He did for women. Before Christ came, this was a man's world. Only men were happy. They weren't really, they only thought they were. But women and children were not happy, and they knew they were not happy. For men mistreated them and abused them and ignored them and exploited them. Women wore sad faces before Christ came into the world. And little children, too, were sad and dreary. But Christ changed all that. He made men and women and children happy. He brought happiness to all the world. He turned children from little, unwanted, half-starved, mistreated slaves into the very Children of God. He brought joy into the world, and not the least of it into the faces and into the voices of little children.

Little children, therefore, should love Christ and serve Him.

CHAPTER XVII

" Lift Ye Up a Banner "
(FLAG DAY)

☙❧

ISAIAH 13: 2: " Lift ye up a banner . . ."

OBJECTS: Small American flags, one of which is to be given to each child as he leaves the service.

☙❧

IN God's Book, in the part of it called the Prophecy of Isaiah, in the 13th chapter and the 2nd verse we find our text: " Lift ye up a banner . . ." That sounds like a flag, doesn't it? And that is what it was. Here in my hand, I lift up a number of little American flags and I am going to give one of these to each boy and girl as he leaves the church this morning as a token for Flag Day. June 14th is the Birthday of our American Flag. That is why we call it " Flag Day."

*   *   *   *   *

When our ancestors came to America, began to settle this new land, and established here some English colonies, they naturally used the British flag. For they were British citizens; they had come, most of them, from the British Isles; they were used to and they loved the British flag. But in addition to that, some of the different colonies wanted to have their own flags also. And so several different flags came to be made and to be used, like the famous flag that bore a pine tree upon it.

But when the Revolutionary War began, the colonies wanted very much to have some kind of a flag that would show plainly that they did not intend to belong to England any longer. So different people in different parts of this country began making flags to show that idea. In Connecticut, for example, they made a flag for that colony. They put on their flag the arms of the colony of Connecticut and a motto in Latin: "He who brought us over sustains us," meaning, of course, that God brought the colonists over to this country and that God would take care of them. In New York or New Amsterdam, the flag that was used had a beaver on it to stand for the industry of the Dutch people who had settled in this state and also the wealth of the fur trade. In New England, the flag often had on it the motto of Massachusetts, "An Appeal to Heaven" and the Pine Tree.

Some ships flew a flag that showed a mailed fist grasping a bundle of thirteen arrows, an arrow for each of the thirteen colonies. In the south there appeared a blue flag, with a white crescent in the upper corner next the staff and carrying the motto: "Liberty or Death." A flag with a rattlesnake was often used; and usually the snake had thirteen rattles and on the flag was the motto: "Don't Tread on Me." At Cambridge, Mass., on Jan. 1, 1776, George Washington used a flag of thirteen red and white stripes with the flag of England, the British Union Jack, in the upper corner. You see how this flag of Washington was a forerunner of the flag we now love so well.

It was on June 14, 1777, during the Revolutionary War, that the Continental Congress passed a resolution: "That the flag of the thirteen United States be thirteen stripes, alternate red and white; that the union be thirteen stars, white in a blue field, representing a new constellation." This gave us, officially, the flag of the United States. Paul Jones was the first man to use the new flag on a naval vessel. And it was first used on land at Fort Stanwix, in our state (New York), when a hastily improvised flag was raised over the fort on August 3, 1777. The thirteen states at that time, each of which had a stripe and each a star in the new flag, were: Delaware, Pennsylvania, New Jersey, Georgia, Connecticut, Massachusetts, Maryland, South Carolina, New Hampshire, Virginia, New York, North Carolina and Rhode Island.

After a while, Vermont and Kentucky were added to the union as new states. So in 1794 the flag was changed to show that these two new states belonged to our country. Two stripes were added and two stars, making the total fifteen stripes and fifteen stars. This is the flag that Francis Scott Key wrote about in our national anthem, "The Star Spangled Banner." Still more states came into the union and by 1818 there were twenty states in the United States. Surely a flag with only fifteen stripes and fifteen stars would not do for a country with twenty states, so the flag was changed again. Now it had thirteen stripes for the original thirteen states and twenty stars for the twenty states at that time, with the understanding that one star was to be added every time a new state should be taken into the country, but that the number of stripes was to remain at thirteen.

Today, you all know, we have forty-eight states in our union and so we have forty-eight stars in our flag. The last stars to be added were in 1912 when New

Mexico and Arizona became states of the union. And that makes the flag as we have it today.

I

This is the flag of the United States of America. Let us be proud of it. It is a great flag and it stands for a great nation.

II

Let us show respect for our flag. Let us learn the proper way to use it, when and how to display it, how to salute it, how to honor and respect it. Let us learn when to put it up and when to take it down, how to keep it from touching the ground, how to lower it after sunset and how to dispose of old, torn and worn-out flags in a reverent and respectful manner. We do not worship the flag or the country it represents. We worship only God Who gave us our country and Who helped us make our flag great. But we do want to show respect for the flag.

III

And let us do all we possibly can to make our country, America, both good and great. We have a wonderful country and a wonderful flag. Let us help make our land even greater and better, nobler and finer, more and more worthy of the beautiful and wonderful flag that is hers.

CHAPTER XVIII

One Red Rose *

(SUMMER)

ରେ ୨ ବ

OBJECT: One red rose in a blue, glass vase.

ରେ ୨ ବ

I HAVE a beautiful story for you, this morning, boys and girls. And to illustrate it, I have in the pulpit with me this lovely red rose in a blue, glass vase.

The story is a true story. And that makes it all the more beautiful. It is about a man whose name was Henry William Stiegel, who came to this country 200 years ago. He was born in Germany but came to the United States when he was twenty-one. He married well. That is to say the lady who became his wife was a woman of good family and of some wealth. Stiegel went into the glass business. There were not many glassmakers in this country in that early day. And Mr. Stiegel's glass was very good and in great demand and he made a real fortune out of it. But, sad to say, he lost his fortune later on; and finally died penniless.

But the glass he left behind him proved to be a great heritage. It was so good and so clear and so beautiful. Today Stiegel glass is very famous and very valuable. It is noted for its exquisite color and collectors seek it and pay large sums to get pieces of it. It is found in various colors: blue, amethyst, green, amber and both clear and opaque white. That means,

* The story of Stiegel was told by Jonathan Fife in the *American Agriculturist* and is used here by gracious permission of the publishers of that journal.

you know, that some of the white is so made that you can see through it while some of it is so made that you cannot see through it.

In 1770 (that was before our Revolutionary War and our Declaration of Independence, you know, a long time ago) he gave a plot of ground to the Zion Lutheran Church in Brickerville, Pennsylvania. Brickerville is in Lancaster County, Pennsylvania, one of the most beautiful farming countries in the whole world. Well, Stiegel gave a plot of land to the church there and he made a strange but beautiful provision when he made the gift. He gave it to the church on condition that the church should pay " one red rose annually in the month of June forever, if the same shall be legally demanded by the heirs, executors or assigns." That was the rent, and the only rent, he asked for the land. It would belong to the church forever, if the church paid him or his family one red rose each year.

And today, almost 200 years afterward, Stiegel's descendants still receive, every June, one red rose. Isn't that a beautiful story? And isn't that a beautiful way for a church to pay rent for the ground it is built on?

I

Mr. Stiegel must have been a great man. To begin with, he loved the beautiful. He created such beautiful glass. And he loved flowers. He loved the beautiful so much that he only asked one red rose as rent for the land he gave to the church. We should cultivate a love for the beautiful.

II

More than that, he loved the church. For if he did

not love the church, God's House, God's people, he would not have given to the church that gift of land and asked nothing in return but one red rose each year! He loved the church and he gave to the church. We should learn to love the church and give to the church.

III

So much for his character. He loved the beautiful and he loved the church. But there is a third lesson for us today from his money. Money can be lost. That is something we should not forget. Money can be lost. Often we lose a little bit, do we not, when we drop a coin in the street and watch it roll away, probably dropping into some gutter and running into a catch-basin out of sight and out of reach? We often lose a little money. But Mr. Stiegel lost a great deal of money; all he had! Money can be lost. And so it is good to remember that it is not what we have that counts in this life, but what we do. It is not the money we have made that makes people remember us. It is the good that we have done. Stiegel is not remembered today for the vast fortune he once made and then lost. He is not remembered for his money. But he is remembered for the wonderful glass he made. His marvelous and valuable glass is his memorial. And so what we do will count. Not what we have.

IV

But even more important than that, we should remember that very often what we give is the best memorial of all. Better than what we have, better than what we do, often what we give is the thing that people remember us by. The land that this famous glass-maker gave to the church is his best memorial, after all. It is remembered, this gift of his, every year, by the rose. Every year that whole church and the whole countryside round about remembers Henry William Stiegel when the church pays one red rose to his family. They remember him for what he gave.

CHAPTER XIX

The Liberty Bell

(INDEPENDENCE DAY)

LEVITICUS 25: 10: "Proclaim liberty throughout all the land unto all the inhabitants thereof."

OBJECTS: Pictures of the Liberty Bell to be distributed to the children either before the Children's Sermon or as they leave the church. "The Perry Pictures" are inexpensive or any others may be used.

THE ushers are giving to every boy and girl in church this morning a picture of the Liberty Bell. I want you to look at the picture as I tell you something about the bell in this, our Fourth of July Sermon, for it is one of the most famous bells in all the world. The text for our Children's Sermon is the text that is cast into the side of the famous old bell. It is a wonderful text, from God's Word, the Book of Leviticus, the 25th chapter and the 10th verse: "Proclaim liberty throughout all the land unto all the inhabitants thereof."

The Liberty Bell was made in England and shipped

to America in 1752 to be used in the State House in Philadelphia. It was not called the Liberty Bell then, of course, for it was not yet famous. It was a very ordinary bell indeed and was sent over to Philadelphia to be used in the building that was the headquarters of the government of the British Colony of Pennsylvania. But the bell was probably not made exactly correctly for it had to be recast, that is, made over. So it was melted up and recast in April and then once again in June of 1753. And it was at this time, when it was recast in America, that the text from the Bible was put upon it. That text read, as we have just seen: " Proclaim liberty throughout all the land unto all the inhabitants thereof." Now that was in 1753, many years ago.

In 1776, you know, the Declaration of Independence, which announced to all the world that this country was free and independent and no longer belonged to England, was adopted in that very same old building, the State House in Philadelphia, in whose tower the old bell hung. On July 4, 1776, the Declaration of Independence was adopted and that great, old bell in the tower of the State House was rung. It was rung long and loud and its notes swelled out over the city to announce the good news. It was the first bell to ring out in celebration of the independence of this land, in celebration of the Declaration of American Liberty. And so it came to be called, " The Liberty Bell." And every year after that, it was rung, long and lustily, on July 4th, the birthday of the American Republic. Every year on July 4th it rang out to celebrate our independence, to declare our liberty.

It was also used on other occasions, of course. And

finally on July 8, 1835, it cracked when it was being rung in memory of Chief Justice Marshall of the United States Supreme Court. A great crack appeared in its side and so the famous, old bell was silenced. No longer could it ring. But, do you know, the crack in the old bell soon became as famous as the bell itself? And everybody thinks of the Liberty Bell today as the great, old bell with the big crack in it which rang out for independence on July 4, 1776, but does not ring any more. The famous, old bell now hangs in the hallway of the old State House in Philadelphia. The bell is now called, "The Liberty Bell," and the building in which the Declaration of Independence was adopted and signed is no longer called, "The State House," but "Independence Hall."

Now to my mind, the most interesting thing about this old bell is the inscription upon it: "Proclaim liberty throughout all the land unto all the inhabitants thereof." Because you must remember that those words were put on it long before it was used to announce liberty to the land. Those words were put on the bell in 1753 and it was not until 1776 that it was used to do the very thing the text on its side said it ought to do, proclaim liberty to all the land and to all the people who lived in the land. Here was a strange prophecy. Here was put on the side of the bell an idea which many years afterward the bell was used to carry out. When the bell was recast in Philadelphia this text was placed on its side. And many years afterward the text was fulfilled, the prophecy came to pass, and the bell did proclaim liberty on Independence Day, July 4, 1776. And today the Liberty Bell is honored as much as anything that we have in this land of ours.

But one thing more I want you to remember. That text on the side of the bell came from the Bible. Indeed the whole idea of liberty comes from God. God wants men to be happy and God wants men to be free. God put the idea of liberty into the Bible. Some Americans got it out of the Bible and put it on the bell. And at last the bell fulfilled its own prophecy and proclaimed liberty throughout the land. And though its tongue has been silenced, it is still doing that very thing. It is still telling the world that God wants men to be happy and He wants them to be free.

Let us love our country. Let us keep our liberty. Let us praise God for both our country and our liberty. For God gave us America and God helped us make it free.

CHAPTER XX

" *A Mighty Man, But a Leper* "

❧❦❧

2 KINGS 5: 1: "Now Naaman, captain of the host of the king of Syria, was a great man with his master, and honourable, because by him the Lord had given deliverance unto Syria: he was also a mighty man in valour, but he was a leper."

❧❦❧

I THINK that all the boys and girls know the beautiful story of the little captive maid who had been carried away by the soldiers from the Land of Israel into the Land of Syria and had become a servant of the wife of the mighty general of Syria, Naaman. You remember how she was saddened by the fact that Naaman had that dreadful disease, leprosy; and how she told her mistress that Elisha, the mighty prophet in Israel, could cure him if he would but go to him. I think that the story of this little captive maid is one of the most beautiful stories in the Bible. But it is not about the lovely little maid that I want to tell you this morning, but rather about the mighty general, Naaman, and his cure.

I

Naaman was a very great man but he had a very terrible disease. You all know something of what leprosy is and how dreaded it always has been. It was with this terrible disease that Naaman was afflicted.

Sometimes, you know, great men are bowed down by God. Sometimes God brings trouble and disease upon even the greatest of men. That idea is plainly given to us in our text, which is found in the Word of God as it is written in the Second Book of Kings, the fifth chapter and the first verse: " Now Naaman, captain of the host of the king of Syria, was a great man with his master, and honourable, because by him the Lord had given deliverance unto Syria: he was also a mighty man in valour, but he was a leper." He was a great man, a very great man. But he was a sick man, a very sick man. God had sent leprosy upon him. Very often the greatest of men are afflicted, bowed down by God. It was so with Naaman. He was a mighty man, but a leper.

II

But notice, please, that Naaman, this mighty man who was so sick with leprosy, believed the report of the little girl. The little Jewish maid told her mistress about Elisha, the great prophet of Israel, and that he could cure her master if he would but go to him. And Naaman believed what she said and went out of the country of Syria into the country of Israel to find Elisha and ask him to cure him. He believed what the little captive slave girl had said. The mighty general, great in his splendor and his power, believed the report of the little girl who worked in his home, who had been captured and made a slave by his soldiers. A mighty man believed a little girl. And so the poorest of us can testify to Christ, just like this little, poor, dreary slave girl testified to Him in the ancient day long before He was born. The smallest of us, the poorest of us, the

most handicapped of us can tell others about Christ.
She told others about her religion and what it did for
her and her people and what it could do for others. So
can we tell of our religion and what it will do and can
do for other people.

III

And so Naaman went to Israel and saw Elisha and
asked him to cure him. And Elisha told him how God
would cure him. But then Naaman did a very strange
thing. He decided that he would not do the thing that
God wanted him to do to get well. He did not want to
use God's method. Elisha told him how to get well,
how God would cure him. And Naaman, after coming
all that distance to consult the prophet, did not want to
do it. He thought the method of cure that Elisha told
him about was too simple and too easy and therefore
he would not try it. "And Elisha sent a messenger unto
him, saying, Go and wash in Jordan seven times, and
thy flesh shall come again to thee, and thou shalt be
clean." Elisha told him that all he had to do was go
to the River Jordan and wash himself in it seven times
and he would be cured. And Naaman refused to do it
because it was too simple! He wanted a better way to
get cured, a better way than God's. He wanted to be
cured in his own way instead of God's. For this is
what he said: "Are not Abana and Pharpar, rivers of
Damascus, better than all the waters of Israel? may I
not wash in them, and be clean? So he turned and went
away in a rage." He wanted to be cured, but he did not
want to be cured God's way. He wanted to be cured his
own way or not at all. And so he said that they had
better rivers in Damascus than the Jordan in Israel and

he guessed he could go home and bathe in one of them!

And that, boys and girls, is the way it too often is with us. We do not want to use God's method. We prefer our own way to God's way. For many people, the Gospel is too simple and too easy and they do not like it and they turn away from it in a rage. For the Gospel says, "Just believe," and people think that is too easy and too simple and cannot really give them peace and salvation and happiness and joy. They want a better way, they want their own way, they want to work for their salvation, they want to earn their salvation by their deeds or their character, when God tells them that He will give them and all men salvation if they only believe. Such people do not want God's way, they want their own, for God's way seems too simple and easy for them.

IV

But at last Naaman changed his mind and he tried God's way and he was cured. For his servants came to him and said, "My father, if the prophet had bid thee do some great thing, wouldst thou not have done it? how much rather then, when he saith to thee, Wash, and be clean?" If Elisha the prophet had asked him to do some hard thing, Naaman would have done it. Why not at least try this simple thing, so easy, just go down to the river and bathe? Naaman saw that what they said to him was sensible, and that it would be most foolish not at least to try it. "Then went he down, and dipped himself seven times in Jordan, according to the saying of the man of God: and his flesh came again like unto the flesh of a little child, and he was clean." He obeyed God and he was cured. He was saved when he obeyed God fully. And so are we, boys and girls. We are cured of sin, we have the gift of salvation, we are saved when we obey God and believe. Very simple, very easy; easier by far than dipping ourselves in the river seven times. Only believe; believe God; believe in Christ, our Saviour. And when we obey God, we, too, shall be saved.

Let us learn the lesson of Naaman, " a mighty man, but a leper."

CHAPTER XXI

Why Do We Celebrate Labor Day?
(LABOR DAY)

❧❧❧

GENESIS 3: 19: " In the sweat of thy face shalt thou eat bread."

❧❧❧

BOYS and girls, one of the purposes of these Children's Sermons that I give to you from time to time is to get you better acquainted with the Bible, God's Book. And that is why I usually try to give you a text, one of the great, inspiring and familiar texts of the Wonderful Book. Today I have one of the most familiar texts for you, and one of the very greatest. It is found in the first Book of the Bible, Genesis, in the 3rd chapter and the 19th verse, the first part of the verse: " In the sweat of thy face shalt thou eat bread." In this text, God is telling us that we must work for

what we eat; that mankind must labor (that is what
" sweat of thy face " means) in order to make a living
(that is what " shalt thou eat bread " means). It is the
law of nature and it is the law of God that man must
work in order to eat.

Tomorrow is Labor Day and so our text becomes a
Labor Day text, you see. Now, why do we celebrate
Labor Day? We celebrate Labor Day to honor labor
and those who work; to show that we respect both the
work men do and the men who do the work; to make
clear to all that working is proper and right and good
and that men who work are also proper and right and
good. So Labor Day honors both the work men do and
the men who do the work. And since tomorrow is
Labor Day there are some things that I should like
very much to have you boys and girls keep in mind. In
fact, there are three things that I should like very much
to tell you about work or labor.

I

First of all, I want to speak to you about the Dignity
of Labor. Work or labor is dignified. Work is proper,
work is right, work is honorable, work is noble. Never
forget that. Never get to thinking that there is anything wrong or anything dishonorable or anything low
or mean or undignified in honest work. The worker is
honored. It is the slacker or the loafer or the man who
tries to sneak out of honest work or cheat himself out
of it who is despised and scorned. The " self-made
man " is honored in this country. He is the man who
worked himself up from nothing to something, from a
humble start to a noble place in life. We admire the
man who makes something of himself, who works his

way up from poverty to riches or from obscurity to fame. The man who works is honored. The man who is lazy and won't work but prefers to loaf about and let others feed him is looked down upon. It has ever been so. Paul wrote in the Bible, you remember, that " if any would not work, neither should he eat." For work is honorable. Remember the dignity of labor.

II

In the second place remember the Demand of Labor. Work is not only noble. It is also necessary. It is not only right and proper to work. It is absolutely required that we work or we cannot live. In the very earliest of days God made that very clear to men when He said in our text, " In the sweat of thy face shalt thou eat bread." You must work for what you eat. Labor is necessary if man and his family are to live. Man must work if himself, his wife and his children are to eat. This is the demand for labor. If there were no work there would be no life. We must work to live. No family can get along very well for any length of time if the man in the family does not work. For if the head of the house does not labor, the family soon starves or at least is " on the town." You have to work in order to live. And that is another thing that Paul meant when he said " if any would not work, neither should he eat." If you do not work for a living you soon do not have the living. But when you remember the demand of labor, the fact that work is necessary, do not forget, boys and girls, that there are many different kinds of labor. Some men work with their hands. That is manual labor. Other men work with their brains. That is mental labor. And the man who works in the shop or in the factory is not working any harder because he works with his hands than the man in the office or the bank who works with his brains.

III

And the third thing I want you to think about is the Delight of Labor. Work is not only right and proper and noble and dignified. Work is not only absolutely necessary. Work should also be pleasant and enjoyable. Labor should be delightful. Work should be something that we like to do. That is why it is important for people to pick out the kind of work they will enjoy when they make up their minds as to what they want to become in this life. Men and women should enjoy the kind of work they do. Pick out the job that is going to make you happy. This is good advice. And if you cannot pick out the work you will like, then try to like the work you must do. Even if you have to work at something that you did not choose yourself, you can learn to like it and you ought to try to like it. Labor should be pleasant. Work should be enjoyable. If it is not already, you must make it so.

Henry van Dyke, one of America's great poets, has a poem in which he tells us of the delight of labor:

> " This is the Gospel of Labor—
>   Ring it, ye bells of the kirk—
> The Lord of love came down from above
>   To live with the men who work.
> This is the rose that he planted
>   Here in the thorn-cursed soil—
> Heaven is blessed with perfect rest;
>   But the blessing of earth is toil." *

* My sincere thanks are extended to Charles Scribner's Sons for their gracious permission to quote this poem.

On Labor Day can you remember three things—the Dignity of Labor, the Demand of Labor and the Delight of Labor?

CHAPTER XXII

" Quit You Like Men, Be Strong "

❧ ☙ ❧

1 CORINTHIANS 16: 13: "Watch ye, stand fast in the faith, quit you like men, be strong."

❧ ☙ ❧

THE text for the boys and girls this morning is found in God's Word, which is the Bible, in the first letter of Paul to the Corinthians, the sixteenth chapter and the thirteenth verse, "Watch ye, stand fast in the faith, quit you like men, be strong." Paul, the greatest missionary of all times and one of the very greatest men who ever lived, was writing a letter to his many friends in the ancient city of Corinth, in Greece. And in his letter he was giving them some advice. And some of his advice to them is contained in this text. He told them to watch. He told them to stand fast in the faith. He told them to act like men. That is what "Quit you like men" means. Act like men. Be men. And then he told them to be strong. "Quit you like men, be strong."

Now I think this is a good text for us today because

today is Men's Sunday in our church and in a few moments I am going to preach a special sermon for the men. But I also want to have a special sermon for the boys at the time of the Children's Sermon. And that is why I chose this text. For what better advice can we give to boys than to act like men and to be strong? But just as the women of the church can listen, if they want to, to the men's sermon after a while, so the girls are going to be permitted to listen to the boys' sermon now. And I hope the advice that I give to the boys will have a meaning for the girls, too. Because if the boys read this text like this, "Act like grown men, not like babies; be strong," surely the girls could read it something like this, "Act like grown women, not like little babies; be strong." For boys want to be men and girls want to be women. And so Paul told his friends in Corinth to act grown up, to act like men and women, to be strong. And just so I tell you today, act like grown men and women, be strong. "Quit you like men, be strong."

Now if the boys want to be strong like men, and if Paul in our text tells us we ought to be, what might that mean?

I

First of all, a man is strong in physical power. A man can carry a load or lift a burden that would be altogether too great for a boy. A man can do heavy work. He can lift great objects. He can carry great weights. And if we are to give ourselves physical power like that, we must keep ourselves strong and clean that we may grow into the strength of manhood. We must eat the right things. We must avoid the things that will sicken or weaken us. We must avoid cigarettes which take our wind and sap our strength. We must keep our health.

II

In the second place, a man is strong in knowledge. A man knows more than a boy. And so to become like a man, we must grow in knowledge. Every boy who is worth his salt thinks his father knows everything. I can well remember my own thoughts along this line when I was a boy. I used to think that my father knew all there was to know about everything on the earth. And that is the way a boy ought to think about his father. But to get to that place where we know more than we do now, we must study and we must learn and become strong in knowledge. We must go to school to learn. That is what the school is for, to make us strong in knowledge like men. We must study the Bible, the greatest Book in the world, to grow in knowledge and become strong.

III

In the third place, a man is strong in courage. A man who is a man, and not a mollycoddle, is not afraid of danger. He has courage and not fear. A man who is a man will stand for the right even when it is hard work and dangerous to stand for the right. This is courage. Courage in face of danger and courage in face of wrong both belong to men who are worthy of the name of men. And it is God who will give us this courage.

IV

And in the fourth place, a man is strong in faith.

The first part of our text says so: "Watch ye, stand fast in the faith." Stand fast in the faith. A man who is a man is strong in the faith. He stands fast in it. A real man believes in Christ. A real man accepts Him as his Saviour. A real man trusts in Him. A real man has faith. We are to have faith, boys and girls, always. We may not know much about the Christian religion. We are only boys and girls still. But we can have faith, just the same. We can know what we do know. We can know that Christ loves us. We can know that Christ died for us. We can know that in return we love Christ. We may not know it all but we do know, as boys and girls, this much at least. Each one of us can say for himself: "Christ loves me. Christ died for me. I will love and follow Him." A man is strong in faith.

"Quit you like men, be strong." If you are to be men, you must be strong in physical power, strong in knowledge, strong in courage, strong in faith. "Quit you like men, be strong."

CHAPTER XXIII

A Great Discoverer

(COLUMBUS DAY)

❧

HEBREWS 11: 8: "By faith . . . he went out, not knowing whither he went."

OBJECTS: Small pictures of Van der Lyn's famous painting, "Landing of Columbus," to be distributed to the children either before the Children's Sermon or as the children leave the church. "The Perry Pictures" issue an inexpensive copy of this famous painting.

❦

THE ushers are giving a copy of a very famous painting to each boy and girl present this morning. It is Van der Lyn's "Landing of Columbus." Look at it a moment. This famous painting is supposed to represent the great discoverer, Christopher Columbus, as he first landed on American soil; as he, and his men, first set foot on the land of the new world which he had discovered. With flags and swords in hand; with some of the men kneeling and some standing; with some of them touching the land in great delight, for they had not stood on solid ground for many weary days; with the savage red men in the background; with the cross above their heads; Columbus and his men are claiming this land for Ferdinand and Isabella, King and Queen of Spain. I am giving you this picture and asking you to keep it because this week our country celebrates Columbus Day, remembering that on October 12, 1492, Columbus first set foot on American soil. It was a very wonderful thing that Columbus had done and well might we celebrate the anniversary of his landing.

There is a text in the Bible, a grand text, which of course was not written about Columbus but which describes him pretty well just the same. It is found in the book of Hebrews, the 11th chapter and the 8th verse. We take the first two words of the verse, skip the whole middle part of it and then take the very last of it and this is what we read: "By faith . . . he went out, not knowing whither he went." Now that fits Columbus very well. For there is an old saying about him that runs something like this. Columbus did not know where he was going when he set out from Spain on that wonderful voyage that gave a whole new world to men. And when he got to this side of the ocean he did not know where he was. When he got back home again he did not know where he had been. And he did it all on somebody else's money! That fits Columbus very well. For he did not know where he was going. He did not know where he was when he got there. He did not know where he had been when he got back. And he did do it all on somebody else's money. The King and Queen of Spain paid for his voyage, of course.

But even though that is perfectly true about Columbus, it is also true that he was a great man and a great discoverer. He did think he was going some place else. He did not know what land it was when he landed in the West Indies, on a tiny island off the coast of North America. He was not sure where he had been when he got home. The King and Queen of Spain did pay his expenses. But just the same he was a great discoverer and his voyage gave a whole new hemisphere to the world, two whole new continents, North and South America. Because he made that memorable voyage, America was discovered; America was given to the world.

Now Columbus had courage to do that thing, great courage. And we must always think of him as a man of courage. No man had sailed across that great sea before him, unless it was Leif Ericson who came across the northern part of it years before from Denmark and Iceland and Greenland. But if he had done it he left no record of it and nobody at Columbus's time knew anything about it. So, as far as he or any other man knew, it was something entirely different that Columbus was doing. He set out across an unknown sea. No man could tell him for sure what lay across it. He had no sure idea of what land he would find, of what kind of people he might meet, of what kind of hardships he might run into. He did not know the ocean currents; he had no knowledge of the winds that might blow his vessels to pieces; he had no charts to show the shallows and the reefs; he knew nothing of the life on the lands he might reach. And worst of all, his sailors, superstitious and rebellious, were afraid and wanted to turn around and go home. It took great courage to set out on such a voyage and it took great courage to keep it up and to carry it through. Columbus was a man of courage.

And also Columbus had great faith. He was a man of faith, great, wonderful faith. Now that is why I said a few moments ago that we could apply our text to him. This great text is really about Abraham, the father and the founder of the mighty Hebrew race into which Jesus Christ, the Saviour of the world, was later born. And our text tells us that when Abraham was called by God to go into a new land and found a new nation which in turn would bring a blessing upon all the world, he left his home and his father's country and went out to a new land, not even knowing where it was he was going. It took faith to do that, great faith in God. And that is what our text says of Abraham. He believed in God and he obeyed God. " By faith . . . he went out, not knowing whither he went." It was exactly so with Columbus. " By faith . . . he went out, not knowing whither he went."

Columbus, too, was a man of faith. Faith, belief in God, trust in his religion was one of the things that really sent Columbus out to find the new world. We say it was a religious urge that sent him forth after all. Because he wanted to spread his religion. That is one of the chief reasons for his going. He wanted to spread his religion to new lands and to new peoples. It is true that his religion was a different form of Christianity from our own, but it was Christianity just the same. And he wanted to give it to new people in new lands. And this religious idea had much to do with his starting and his finishing his famous voyage.

Religion, you see, was really the start of our nation. Columbus had a religious reason for coming here. He wanted to spread Christianity. The Pilgrims, 130 years later, came to America for religious reasons, to find a place where they could worship God according to the dictates of their own consciences. Much of the history of our country has had religion back of it. Much of the glory of America has been due to our religion. Let us keep America not only a free country but a religious one!

CHAPTER XXIV

The Painted Tree

(FALL)

❧

GENESIS 2: 9 : " And out of the ground made the Lord God
to grow every tree that is pleasant to the sight, and good
for food."

OBJECT: A colored maple leaf.

❧

THE text for the boys and girls on this beautiful fall
day is found in the Word of God as it is written in
the Book of Genesis, the second chapter and the ninth
verse: " And out of the ground made the Lord God to
grow every tree that is pleasant to the sight, and good
for food." In this text, the Bible tells us that God made
the trees to grow out of the ground and that they are
beautiful to look at and that many of them produce
some of the food that we eat. We all know how much
of our food comes from trees—nuts, fruits, maple
sugar. But it is the first part of the text that I want to
think about especially today, the part that says that
God made the beautiful trees to grow to be " pleasant
to the sight." Because I want to tell you about a
painted tree this morning.

In the fall of the year the leaves on the trees turn.
You all have noticed, I am sure, how beautiful the
trees become at this season. I am sure that nobody can
look at a lovely maple tree, all brilliant and magnificent in its fall coloring, without thinking of God Who

made the trees so " pleasant to the sight." Most of the trees, except the evergreens, display many wonderful colors on their leaves at this time of the year, but possibly the maples are the most beautiful of all. The other day, while out in the country, I saw a wonderful sight. It was a huge maple tree, standing alone in a field. Most of the tree was still green—the entire center portion having its leaves one solid color, dark, luxuriant green. But the tips of every limb were touched with red. Every branch proudly displayed a number of bright, red leaves! A green tree with red trimmings—a green tree tipped with red. It looked as if some master artist had touched every branch with red paint. Indeed it was a painted tree. For a Master Artist had given it its color. And that Master Artist was God.

Coming back to town that day, I saw another tree, just as beautiful, just as truly painted, but very different from the green tree trimmed with red. For this second tree that I beheld was all red, like a huge flame bursting out of the ground. This red tree I saw in our Park and it looked for all the world like a blazing fire rising up out of the ground in the midst of the other trees. In another place, along the road, I saw a tree with still a different color. This one was one solid mass of yellow —a beautiful sight, a tree bathed in gold!

The other day I saw still a different sight. I was driving home from Delaware County and was coming out of the famous Catskill Mountains. And as I drove up a certain long hill, in a locality called Meredith, I saw a great row of trees growing all along the roadside. And by some freak of nature these trees had been touched by the change of fall in a most unusual and interesting way. For this long row of maples consisted of trees in alternate colors, red, yellow and green. I mean the first tree was all red, the second was all yellow, the third had not yet changed and so was all green; the fourth was all red, the fifth all yellow, the sixth all green; and so on and so on up that long rise of ground along the highway. Painted trees, all of them, yet in such regular order, so symmetrical, so beautiful. And then, a little farther along my way, I saw another picture, very different from that one, yet just as beautiful and just as glorious and just as truly designed to make me think of God, the Author of so much beauty. This picture was a hillside that rose up before my wondering eyes; a hillside literally covered with a riot of color. It was thickly wooded and the mass of trees were all different colors. Some were still green, the pines and the hemlocks and the others that had not yet turned. Some were red, some yellow, some brown, some red and yellow and brown all mixed together. One vast hillside covered with a tremendous mass of color. Everywhere color, everywhere beauty, everywhere the handiwork of God the Master Artist.

There is so much beauty in the world. If you look for it, you can find it everywhere, especially in the fall. And seeing all this beauty, unless you are blind in your soul, you cannot help but think of God. God put all this beauty in the world. God makes the world magnificent every day, especially in the fall. But why does God do it? *For our pleasure.* God makes the world beautiful for us to enjoy. He wants men and women and boys and girls to see the beauty all around them, to think of Him who gave it to them, and to be happy in it. God wants us to be happy! There is no other reason for the beauty of the earth. There can be no other reason. That is why He made the trees so " pleasant to the sight." That is why He made the world so beautiful. It didn't need to be so beautiful. It could exist without being beautiful. Mankind could live in it even if it were not so beautiful. But God wants us to be happy, because God loves us! What a wonderful thought! What a wonderful God!

Now if God gives us all this beauty to enjoy, if God makes the world so beautiful just to make us happy, how can we say, " Thank You," to God? How can we tell Him we are grateful? How can we show Him we appreciate what He has given us to enjoy? By doing what He wants us to do! That is the answer. That is the way. We can say, " Thank You," to God by doing what He wants us to do!

CHAPTER XXV

The Illuminated Waterfalls

GENESIS 1: 3: " And God said, Let there be light: and there was light."

JOHN 1: 5: " And the light shineth in darkness; and the darkness comprehended it not."

REVELATION 22: 5: " And there shall be no night there; and they need no candle, neither light of the sun; for the Lord God giveth them light: and they shall reign for ever and ever."

B OYS and girls, I have three texts for you this morning. They are interesting texts for each one is about light but they come from different parts of the

Bible. The first one is from the very first book of the Bible and the very first chapter, Genesis, chapter 1 and verse 3: " And God said, Let there be light: and there was light." The second text is from the Gospel according to John, the first chapter and the fifth verse: " And the light shineth in darkness; and the darkness comprehended it not." The third text is from the very last book in the Bible and from the very last chapter, Revelation, chapter 22 and verse 5: " And there shall be no night there; and they need no candle, neither light of the sun; for the Lord God giveth them light: and they shall reign for ever and ever." The first of these three texts, you see, tells us that God made the light. The second one tells us that God sent light into the world when He sent His Son, Jesus Christ, into the world. And the third text tells us that God will give light to His people in heaven.

These three texts from three different parts of the Bible speak about light and all tell us that God gives it to us. So the Bible has much to say about light. The Bible speaks about light in the very first chapter of the very first book. At the very beginning of the Gospel, we read about light. That is what it means when it says that the light shineth into the darkness; Jesus Christ came into the dark and gloomy world. The beginning of Christ's life was marked by the coming of light into the world. And the very last chapter of the very last book of the Bible speaks again of light, the light that God will give to His people in eternity.

Now the subject that I want to speak to you about this morning is " The Illuminated Waterfalls "; light that shines on some beautiful waterfalls that I have seen.

One of these is in Switzerland. It is called the Trümmelbach Falls and is located in the mountains near the
beautiful city of Interlaken. It is difficult to describe
the great beauty and the great force of these lovely
falls. A huge volume of water dashes down a rocky
gorge in the mountainside. In one place the water
rushes out of a large hole in the rocky wall of the
mountain; in another place the water dashes down a
narrow gorge with the rocks of the Alpine hills meeting overhead. In one place the water dashes 100 feet
or more into a narrow channel. Part of the way you
can walk along the dashing stream on a narrow ledge,
where the rocky sides of the tiny gorge are close together and where the overhanging rocks meet above
your head and form a roof. In these places, where the
rocks overhead meet and roof in the narrow gorge
carrying the dashing stream, it would be very dark indeed if it were not for the bright, colored electric lights
that illuminate the passages. Pink and blue lights have
been erected here and there to light the path. And
they shine down into the rushing water, making it a
thing of beauty, with pinks and blues chasing each
other along the surface of the dashing stream. The waterfall is lighted by electricity and becomes a shimmer-
ing thing of exquisite beauty.

There is another famous waterfall that is illuminated by electricity. This one is in America. We call it
Niagara Falls and every American is proud of it and
loves it. Really, I suppose, it is the most famous waterfall in the world. There are really two great falls at
Niagara, besides several smaller ones; the American
Falls and the Canadian or Horseshoe Falls, with a
great island in between. A mighty volume of water

drops headlong over these two mighty cataracts 160 feet into the gorge below. At night, hundreds of colored flood lights are directed upon the thundering water as it dashes over the edge of the cliff and forms the falls. Attendants change the color of the lights and so now the water looks all pink, now all blue, now all yellow. All through the evening the wonderful lights are thrown upon the water and the most wonderful combinations of colors are produced. I remember very well one time sitting with my family on a balcony of a famous restaurant on the Canadian side of the river and seeing the changes of the wonderful lights play upon the falls. A thing of beauty. A thing of wonder. A thing of great power and force and volume

I

It is God Who gives us beauty, boys and girls. Who but God carved out that deep, narrow gorge down which thunders the Trümmelbach Falls in the mighty Alps? Who but God directed that tremendous volume of water that drains the Great Lakes over the mighty cliff that forms the majestic and awe-inspiring Niagara Falls? Why are these magnificent waterfalls in the world, but to give beauty to the world and to make men praise God Who made such beautiful things? God gives us beauty. God gives us power. For those same falls are powerful things. One is amazed at the tremendous force that is packed in the rushing water. God gives us light. The light of the sun, the light of the Gospel, the light that that very tumbling water can generate are all gifts of God. Nobody who has any soul can behold Trümmelbach Falls without thanking God for beauty and for power and for light. Nobody who has any soul can stand before Niagara without raising a prayer to God for His goodness and His mercy.

II

But, and here is a very interesting thing, it is the power that is made by Niagara Falls, that is used to illuminate it! Great power houses line the banks of the Niagara River on both sides. And these power houses use the force of the mighty falls to generate electricity, thousands and thousands of horse-power being made every day. Now it is the very electricity that the falls make that in turn is used to light them at night! The power from Niagara illuminates Niagara!

Do you know what that makes me think of? It makes me think that our work for God will reward us. The work we do for God will bring glory to us. God asks us to work for Him. There is much we are to do for Him. And we do it for Him and not for ourselves. But the point of it is, that while we do it for Him and for His glory, it will also, at the same time, reward us. It will give us power, it will give us light, it will give us glory.

There is an old hymn your parents used to like to sing. It tells about the reward of the Christian life. And the chorus runs:

" O that will be glory for me,
Glory for me, glory for me;
When by His grace I shall look on His face,
That will be glory, be glory for me." *

* Copyright, 1928, renewal. Homer A. Rodeñeaver, owner. My sincere thanks go to The Rodeheaver, Hall-Mark Company for permission to quote this chorus.

Yes, there is a glory in the Christian life. And our work for God brings it to us.

CHAPTER XXVI

The Broken Telephone Pole

❦

GALATIANS 6: 5: "For every man shall bear his own burden."

❦

Boys and girls, your text today is a good one and a short one. And it fits perfectly the true story I am going to tell you. It is taken from the Letter to the Galatians, the sixth chapter and the fifth verse: "For every man shall bear his own burden." Now think carefully and watch closely and you will discover exactly how this text fits in with the story.

The other day I took a carload of young people to Canton to a Christian Endeavor meeting. On the way we noticed a telephone pole beside the road that had been broken off at the bottom but was still hanging in position from the wires. Some car had probably had an accident at that spot and had run into that pole and snapped it off near the ground. But it had not been wrenched away from the wires and so the wires still held it in place. The string of poles that lined the State Highway at that point held up a large number of wires and when this one particular pole was broken off at the bottom there were enough wires overhead to hold it up. The entire bottom part of the pole was gone, but there it hung, suspended some distance above the ground, hanging from the wires overhead.

Now that pole had been put there in the first place to hold up the wires. But it was now broken and useless and the wires were holding it up. It was supposed to hold up the telephone wires but instead the wires were holding the pole up. But what held the wires up? Why, the other poles, of course. The other nearby poles held up the wires and the wires in turn held up the broken pole. That meant, do you see, that the other poles were doing the work that they were supposed to do and the work of the broken pole as well? And besides all that, they were holding up the broken pole! That pole was not only not doing its work, but it was being held up by other poles that were doing their work, and its work, too.

Now I wonder if you boys and girls can guess what I thought of as soon as I saw that pole not doing its work. I thought at once that that pole was exactly like some people. Don't you know that some people are like that, letting other people do the work they are supposed to do; letting other people carry the whole load, a part of which they ought to carry; letting other people do double work; letting other people carry their own loads and the load that the shirker ought to carry and sometimes the shirker himself, as well? Some people let others do their work for them. Sometimes a person lets other people carry his load for him and then climbs on the load and lets the others carry him, too? Isn't that selfish? Isn't that shirking? Isn't that mean? Isn't that deceitful? Don't you do that, my young friends. Do your own work. Take your own part. Carry your own load. "For every man shall bear his own burden." There is where the text comes in and I have given it away, haven't I?

Now this ideal and this text both apply to all departments of our life. This is a good rule in the home, for example. Do your part in your home, boys and girls. There is a work for each of you to do, I am sure. Do it. Tend to it. Don't be carried along by the other members of the family. Don't let them do their own work and yours, too. That would be like the telephone pole letting the other poles do their work and its, too. Do your part in the home. Don't let others carry you along.

Do your part in school. There is something for each of you to do in school; many things! Your part and your teacher's part and the part of all the other pupils combine to make the school go. Unless all work together and each does his part, the school cannot accomplish its work. Do your share. Do it well. Do it on time. Don't let the others do your work as well as their own and carry you along.

Do your part in church. There is a part for everybody to do in church and Sunday School. Do it! Take your place in the services. Do your part in the worship. Join in the singing and the responsive readings. Do your part in the Sunday School class. There is something for each one to do to make the church and the Sunday School successful. Find your place. Do your part. Don't be carried along by others who do their own work and yours, too. Find your part. Do it!

CHAPTER XXVII

Football

(FALL)

❦

MATTHEW 10: 5: " These twelve Jesus sent forth, and commanded them."

OBJECT: A football.

❦

I WANT to talk to the boys and girls this morning
about football, that great American game that in-
terests so many people in our country in the fall of the
year. Everywhere, these days, we hear people talking
about football. The radio is full of it. The newspapers
are full of it. Our colleges and our high schools are
busy week by week with football games. And everywhere great cheering throngs gather to see games of
this great American sport. Our high school has a football team and we are proud of the team and like to see
them play against other high schools. The colleges our
brothers and sisters go to all have football teams and
it is a great privilege for us to see one of these college
teams play the game.

But did you know that Jesus, when He was on earth,
appointed a *team?* Our text tells us about it. It is found
in Matthew, the tenth chapter and the fifth verse:
" These twelve Jesus sent forth, and commanded
them." Jesus appointed twelve men and sent them
forth to do a certain thing. They were not chosen to
play football. There were twelve of them and not

eleven, as in a modern football team, but they were a team just the same. They were appointed by Jesus to do something for Him and to do it together, as a team does things together.

Now there are many interesting things about football. And I think that if we consider them a moment this morning they will have something to say to us about the game of life.

I

First of all, when you see a football game, you are impressed, I am sure, by the fact that each player on the team must work with the other players on the team. That is what we call "*Team-work*." Each player must co-operate with every other one or the team cannot hope to win. They must all work together to bring about the plays that will help them win the game. A player on a football team cannot go alone at his business. He must consider what every other player on the team is supposed to do and do his part along with them. In fact there really isn't any game in which a player can go all alone without regard to the other players (unless it should be swimming where a boy or a girl is all alone in his sport or tennis or croquet in which there might be just one player on a side). But when you are playing a game with others on a team, you have to work with them; you cannot go at it alone with no regard to the others playing with you; you must use team-work. Your ability at the game is not enough. You must play *with* others.

For example, a football player might be a very good runner. But his running is not enough unless he uses it with the other players on the team. A player might be a very good kicker. But his kicking is not enough unless he uses it in the game with the other members of the team. He cannot just go kicking the ball all over the field without regard to the others playing with him. He would never win the game that way. There must be team-work. They must all work together. Each player has a certain job to perform, a certain work to do. Each one depends on the others. One player cannot walk off with the whole game.

And so it is in life. We must learn to work with others if we would win in the game of life. We cannot live our lives all alone and get anywhere with them. We must practice team-work.

II

But in the second place, there is something in a football game that you must have noticed, that is very characteristic of the game and very necessary for success to any team playing it. It is what we call interference. Now interference in a football game simply means helping a player who is making the play. For example, suppose one man on the team is carrying the ball and running with it for all he is worth. Other members of the team try their best to keep the players on the opposing team from stopping the runner who is carrying the ball. They tackle the opposing players to keep them from tackling their teammate who is carrying the ball and making the play. And if they did not help him, if they did not get the way open for him and keep it open, he could not make the run nor succeed in completing the play. It is not one player's game. It takes the whole team to make the play, even though only one man carries the ball.

And exactly so, it must be in the great game we call life. If we are going to play the game to win, we must be willing to *help another* accomplish something, even if he gets all the *glory*. Many times the spectators at a football game only notice the man who is carrying the ball or making the play and he gets the glory, but it is the whole team that makes the play possible. So it is in life. Very often we must help another person do something really great and good, even if we ourselves do not get the credit nor bask in the glory. But that is the way we play the game to win. That is team-work.

III

A third thing about football is the fact that the game is no good unless fair play dominates it all the way through. You remember how very careful the officials of a game are that both teams play the game fairly and squarely. Fair play is the keynote in a good football game. Neither team must do anything unfair. For if it does, it gets punished for it; or, as the officials say, penalized. Neither team must do anything that it would not want the other team to do. That is what we call fair play. That is practicing the Golden Rule. You remember the Golden Rule that Jesus gave to us. " Therefore all things whatsoever ye would that men should do to you, do ye even so to them." That is the most important rule in football, that rule Jesus gave to us.

But it is also a most important rule in the great game we call life. Use fair play. Don't do to others what you would not want others to do to you. But do to others what you would want them to do to you. Practice the Golden Rule. *Play the game.*

CHAPTER XXVIII

A Real Letter About an Airplane Flight Across the Continent *

❧

B OYS and girls, we live in a wonderful world. God made it and God made us in such a fashion that we can enjoy it and subdue it and control it. And one of the wonderful things that God has given us to help us use and subdue the world is the knowledge of how to fly in the air. By the brains and the hands that God has given to man, we have finally worked out the science of flying like birds. And today we can fly in an airplane all the way across this vast country of ours. Every day regular trips are being made by great fleets of airplanes up and down and across the United States. We owe all that we have to God Who gave us our hands and arms to work with and our minds to think with.

I am going to read to you this morning a real letter that my brother sent to his children, written while he was in one of these great flying ships, crossing our vast country. This letter tells us much about the flight. And this letter also gives the children some good advice. Note this advice and see if it cannot be used by you, too. Here is the letter:

* This chapter and the one following it consist of actual letters written by my brother, Major Lemuel B. Schofield, to his children. I read them to my Junior Congregation because they so vividly describe his transcontinental flight. My thanks go to him for permission to print them in this volume.

In Flight between
Harrisburg & Pittsburgh,
Wednesday, 12:15 P. M.

DEAR JOE:

As you are the oldest, you will receive the first letter,
but I want you to share it with your brother and your sisters
and read it to them too, for it is intended for you all. I think
it would be nice to let Mother see it also, don't you?

I am writing this 2,000 feet up in the air. Just think of
it! Here we are sitting in an airplane, warm and comfortable,
flying rapidly away up above the earth—over the tops of
houses, rivers, towns and cities—much higher than the highest trees or the tallest buildings. We stopped at Harrisburg
(the capital of Pennsylvania) about a half hour ago and in
about an hour we will be in Pittsburgh, which is at the ex-
treme western end of our state. It would have taken all day
or all night to reach there on a train.

I am writing this on a little table in the form of a tray,
which they fasten to the seat. We have just finished our
lunch, which they served to us in a neat little lunch box on
the little table. Here is what each one had to eat:

1 small ham sandwich on white bread,
1 small tongue sandwich on white bread,
1 small chicken sandwich on white bread,
1 hard boiled egg removed from the shell,
1 olive,   1 pickle,   3 stalks of celery,
Hot coffee served from a thermos bottle with cream **and**
    sugar if wanted,
1 piece of cake with black walnuts in it,
Mixed fruit cut up in a paper cup,
A large raw apple,
3 after-dinner mints in a little envelope with a toothpick.

I think that is a good lunch to have up in the air.

We have just passed over a town called Johnstown. It is a
pretty town in a deep valley beside a stream. Once years ago,
a dam across that stream, further up the valley, broke and
the water rushed down the valley and flooded the town and

many people were drowned. As we passed over it, I could see a school 'way below and I wondered how you did in school today. I hope you did well. I know you can if you try.

When we started from Camden this morning, there were nine passengers—two ladies and seven men including myself. Three got off at Harrisburg and no one got on, so there are now but six of us. There are two men who operate the plane, called a pilot and a co-pilot. They sit up front in a little place where the machinery is and they steer the plane with a wheel like the driver of an automobile has.

It is warm in here and everyone takes off his coat and hat. The seats are nice and roomy and very comfortable. At night, they push back and the passenger can lean back and go to sleep as though he were in bed—or at least as though he were home in his " easy chair."

Between Harrisburg and Pittsburgh we pass over three mountain ranges. They are called (in order from east to west) the Blue Ridge Mountains, the Tusey Mountains and the Allegheny Mountains. The last are the highest. They run in long ranges from northeast to southwest, with valleys in between. Of course, the trees are bare at this time of year, but you can tell that the country is very wild, with not many houses or cultivated fields and farms.

One of the most interesting things is to look down and see the shadow of the plane as it races along over the ground. It is shaped like our plane, of course, and you can see it rushing over ploughed fields, across hills and forests, right through houses and barns—always on a straight line and going very fast. You can tell the speed of the plane in this way.

Perhaps you will find it hard to read some of this. It is because every now and then the wind blows the plane up or down or tips it and it is then hard to write.

Give my love to Mother and to Honey, Buddy and little, sweet Lamby. Will you please send this letter to your grandmother to read?

With love,
Your father.
Be a good boy.

CHAPTER XXIX

Another Letter About the Flight

∽◯∾

BOYS and girls, I told you last week that we live in a wonderful world and that we owe all its wonder and all its beauty to God, Who made it. I told you that one of the things that showed us how wonderful our world is, is the fact that we can fly all the way across the United States, if we want to, in an airplane —3000 miles—and that regular trips are made by the great commercial air transport companies every day. I read you a letter that my brother wrote, on such a flight, to his children. Today I am going to read you a second letter that he wrote, because, like the first one, it tells us so much that is interesting about such a flight across the continent.

> In Flight between
> St. Louis and Kansas City,
> Missouri,
> Wednesday, 9 P. M.

DEAR HONEY:

You are the next to the oldest and so you get the second letter, but remember it is to be shared with all the others, especially Mother.

In the first place, perhaps you do not know that as one travels in a westerly direction he loses time. By that is meant that the sun travels west and as one goes with it the light remains longer. So while I have put nine o'clock at the beginning of this letter and it is nine o'clock with you and you are now in bed and, I hope, sound asleep, out here it is only eight o'clock according to their time here.

But whether it is eight or nine does not matter really, for we are flying in the dark and have been for several hours. It is great fun in the dark for you cannot tell how high you are except guessing from lights you see once in a while away down far below. It is fun to go over towns at night and see the many lights below and the automobiles going along the roads with their headlights on. They look like little toy automobiles, and the houses like little toy houses and barns, like we have under the Christmas tree every Christmas time.

But it is just as safe to fly at night as it is in the daytime. The reason is because they have towers with lights on them all along the way—every few miles—and these lights flash on and off or search the sky with their beams, just as in the ocean there are lighthouses and light-ships to tell the captains of the boats where they are. And at the cities where we go down to the ground and land, they have great big lights called " flood lights " which light up the landing field and make it as bright almost as daytime.

In the plane there is a little light over each seat, something like the light beside the seat in the car we sleep in when going to Grandmother's on the train. There are also several lights in the ceiling of the plane and so in here it is nice and bright so that I can write to you.

I am once more writing on the little tray which fits in to my seat, for we have just finished supper. Here is what we had:

> I small chicken sandwich,
> I small roast beef sandwich,
> I small tongue sandwich,
> 1 small cheese sandwich,
> 1 small piece of cake,
> Very hot and good coffee,
> 1 pickle,
> 1 orange,
> 1 hard boiled egg.

They also have sugar in a little paper envelope, and salt and some mints to eat afterwards. It all tasted very good. The sandwiches were each on white bread and each was in a little paper bag of its own, and all of it in a cardboard box.

There are only four passengers now. All the others got off at St. Louis. There were two ladies who got on at Indianapolis and went as far as St. Louis. They were older ladies and there was a younger man with them. He got sick on the way. Many people get sick in an airplane until they get accustomed to flying in the air. The reason is that the wind sometimes blows the plane around so and up and down, especially down—that it bobs up and down like a boat tossed about by the waves—and this at times makes some people ill. It is like what they call, "seasickness," but it is called, "airsickness." I heard one of those ladies say to a man who met her when she got off at St. Louis,—"My! That was just like taking a trip on a ship across the ocean." Luckily it has not affected me as yet.

Of course, sometimes it is worse than other times and when it is very bad they say the air is "*bumpy*" and "rough"— like going over rough places in the road in an automobile. When it is that way you cannot go as fast and if it gets too bad they will not go up at all.

We are an hour behind time now, but this is not because it has been very rough but because all the way from Pittsburgh we have been flying directly against a strong wind which has been blowing against us. This they call a "headwind." My! How fast we would be going if we were going the other way! It will take us over two hours to fly from St. Louis to Kansas City and I heard a pilot say at St. Louis that he had just flown from Kansas City in one hour. You see he was going in the other direction and the wind was behind him blowing him along the faster.

At each stop which we make everybody gets out and walks around a little bit. We usually stay about ten minutes. At Port Columbus we changed planes, but they are both about the same. Isn't that a funny name—"Port Columbus"? It sounds like a city by the sea where the boats land. Perhaps it is because they call airplanes "airships" and "ships."

I hope you are good and all the children are good and well.

122

How is Mother? Is she well? And don't be afraid of the dentist—he won't hurt you.

Will you please send this letter to Aunt Rebecca so she can read it too?

With love to you all,
Your father.

CHAPTER XXX

Thanksgiving Is Giving Thanks
(THANKSGIVING DAY)

❦

EPHESIANS 5: 20: " Giving thanks . . ."

❦

THANKSGIVING DAY will come this week. There is a very good text for Thanksgiving Day in God's Book, in the Letter to the Ephesians, the 5th chapter and the 20th verse. It is also a good text for the Children's Sermon this morning. It says, " Giving thanks . . ." That's our text for today. And that might very well be the text for every family on Thanksgiving Day. " Giving thanks . . ."

The other day I was calling in one of the homes of our congregation. Thanksgiving was coming and the talk naturally turned to that great day of festival and holiday and celebration. There was a little girl in the family who listened to us while we talked. Suddenly she broke in and said, " Thanksgiving? . . . Why you can turn it around—Giving thanks! " And so you can! You can turn Thanksgiving around and make it say " Giving thanks."

Now many, many things can be turned around.

I

And one reason why things can be turned around is to show their real meaning. That is exactly why we ought to turn some things around. For then we shall be able to see what they really mean. And sometimes you do not truly see what a thing means until you do turn it around. But turn it around and its meaning just jumps out at you.

There is, for example, the expression, corn roast—a very popular expression and a very popular thing this time of year. Turn it around to get its meaning and you see that corn roast becomes roast corn. There it is. A corn roast is a party to roast corn. There is hymn sing, another expression we hear much of these days. Turn it around and you get sing hymn, a meeting to sing hymns. Take the sign we see on some stores, shoe repairing. Turn it around and you see you are looking into a shop for repairing shoes. Hair cutting is another sign we often see. Turn it around and you get a shop for cutting hair.

Now that is exactly the way with the expression before us this morning, Thanksgiving. Turn it around to get its real meaning and you find it means giving thanks. That is what it means and that is what it is for. Thanksgiving is giving thanks and Thanksgiving Day is a day for the giving of thanks. On that day we are to give thanks to God. That is what the day is appointed for, to give thanks to God. Let us remember to use it for that purpose. We have much to thank God for. On the day for giving Him thanks let us thank Him for our homes. How good He is to us to give us

our fine, Christian homes. Let us thank Him for our
church. How much it means to us. Let us thank God
for our Sunday School. Let us thank Him also for our
public school. In the Sunday School we learn about
God. In the day school we learn about ourselves and
our world. Let us thank God for our parents, who love
us, who care for us, who do so much for us. Yes, surely
we have much to thank God for on Thanksgiving Day.
And Thanksgiving is giving thanks.

II

But there is a second reason why it is good to turn
things around. The first reason was that thus we can
really know what things mean. The second reason is
that thus we can do to others as we want them to do to
us. Then it is a good thing to turn things around! For
if we turn things around we can do to others just as we
want them to do to us.

For example, if we want people to be kind to us, we
must turn it around and be kind to them. If we want
people to be fair to us, we must turn it around and be
fair to them. If we want people to be honest with us,
we must turn it around and be honest with them. There
are many things that are like that in life. If we want
them done to us, we must do them to others!

And that is true in the matter of giving thanks, too.
We must learn to give thanks to other people when
they do something for us or when they give us something if we want them to thank us for things we do for
them or gifts we give to them. We want others to
thank us for favors. Then we must learn to thank
them for favors done us. This matter of giving thanks
is one of the things that can be and should be turned

around. If we expect people to thank us, we must remember to thank them. It is just as simple as that. And just as important!

For that, boys and girls, is what the Golden Rule is talking about. "All things whatsoever ye would that men should do to you, do ye even so to them."

CHAPTER XXXI

The Baby and the Sunbeam

❦

ISAIAH 60: 1: " Arise, shine."

❦

THE other day I was watching a baby play. He was in a dark place. The only light there was came from two small windows high above his head. Through one of these small windows the bright sun was pouring. As he was playing in the patch of light that came from the window, I noticed that he tried to catch the sunbeam that flung itself like a streak of light through the darkness of that place. You all have noticed how a sunbeam will seem to cut across a dark room like a knife, making a shaft or spear of light that one could almost get hold of. Well, that is just what that baby tried to do—catch that sunbeam. He would run across the room after it; he would clutch his little hand around it; he would think that he was about to grasp it in his tiny fist; and then he would close his hand about the empty air. Over and over again he tried to catch the sunbeam and over and over again he would run after it, grasp out into the air, clutch it and close his hand over nothing.

Watching that baby made me think. Watching other people, old and young, often makes me think. And I thought how foolish that baby was to try to catch such a thing as a sunbeam. He should have known, but of course he did not know, that he could never catch it. He was wasting his time trying to catch something that could not be caught.

I

But, boys and girls, we try to do that sometimes, ourselves, don't we? Don't waste your time trying to catch something you cannot get. You see how foolish it is. And yet boys and girls waste much time trying to catch things they cannot ever get. Sometimes men waste their whole lives trying to catch things they cannot have. Some things you know God doesn't want you to have. Some things you know God just won't let you have. Some things you are not fitted for at all. Don't waste your time trying to get these things. Some of us waste much precious time clutching after things that we can never have, that would hurt us if we got them, that God does not want us to have and that God is not going to let us get. I do not need to name these things. You all know what I mean. Don't waste your time on them.

II

But I want to tell you next that while you cannot catch the sunbeam that shines through the window into a darkened room, you can catch the sunbeam of happiness. And that is worth going after! You can catch happiness if you seek it. If you really grasp after it, if you really clutch after it, you can catch the sunbeam of happiness. And I am going to tell you the secret of happiness, the way to get the sunbeam. It is doing God's will. That is the way to get happiness, to do God's will. Be what He wants you to be. Do what He wants you to do. This is the greatest happiness in the world, after all. Please do not forget that. The way to happiness, the greatest happiness, is to do God's will. There is no happiness greater. People may tell you that there is. You may even at times think there is. But after all is said and done, after all else has been tried, you will discover that this is the greatest happiness that man can know. This happiness will give you a glow of light. That is why I have called it the sunbeam of happiness. And this sunbeam you can get!

III

And finally, I want to say to you, be a sunbeam yourself! Be a gleam of light. Be a bringer of joy. Make others happy. This will be being a sunbeam to them. Show others that you have within you the sunbeam of happiness that comes from doing God's will. And when others see that within you is the sunbeam of happiness, they will look upon you as a sunbeam yourself and you will be bringing peace and light and joy and happiness into their lives. That is what being a sunbeam means. Show the happiness that is yours. Show others that you know Jesus. Show others that you have happiness within you. Be a sunbeam. "Arise, shine." That is what the prophet Isaiah said 700 years before Christ was born. You will find the text in his prophecy, the sixtieth chapter and the first verse. It is good advice for boys and girls today. " Arise, shine." Be a sunbeam.

CHAPTER XXXII

A Light Upon the Path

(UNIVERSAL BIBLE SUNDAY)

PSALM 119: 105: "Thy word is a lamp unto my feet, and a light unto my path."

OBJECT: A flashlight.

How glad we are, boys and girls, for a light on a dark night! If we should be out in the country somewhere, where there are no street lights, or if we should be in town some night when something went wrong with the street lights and they were not shining, how grateful we should be for a flashlight like the one I hold in my hand! If we have to go down the cellar or up into the attic in the dark, or out into the wood-shed or into a dark room, how grateful we are for some light, a candle, a lamp or a flashlight! I want to tell you this morning three true stories about myself to show to you how important a light can be.

Some years ago, when I was a student in the Theological Seminary, I spent one very happy summer near my home in Pennsylvania preaching in two small but very delightful churches in two small but very delightful communities. The town in which I lived was called

Sugar Grove, and a splendid little town it was. But in those days the town had not yet installed electric street lights and after sundown the streets were pretty dark indeed. After church of a Sunday evening, or after some other meeting on some other night, it would be pretty dark getting from the meeting place to your home. Every evening I would see little lights coming along the sidewalks as people out walking would light their paths in front of themselves by the flashlights that they always carried. One night, I remember, after a school entertainment or some such public gathering, a little boy met me on the street crying as if his heart would break. He had lost his parents in the crowd coming out of the meeting and did not know how he would ever get home. And through his tears he asked me if I would not see him safely to his home for he had no light and did not know the way. It was easy enough for me and I took him home in the dark.

Some years after that, when I preached in Hobart, in the Catskill Mountains in southern New York, we had a great storm which put out all the electric street lights one evening. The rain came down in torrents and ran down the streets. The village was plunged into total darkness. And how dark it was on that stormy night out in the rain. I was coming home from a meeting and I had to cross the lovely little bridge that spanned the Delaware River at that point. The Delaware River rose not many miles from that delightful, little mountain village, and its main branch flowed through the town very near the church. I remember groping my way along the street, feeling my way across the bridge, picking my way along the stone sidewalk that I might not miss the way. But just as I got safely across the bridge and came to the point where the stone sidewalk curved away from the bridge, I stepped off the walk and stepped into a deep ditch, full of water, up to my knee! That was a dark and stormy night for you, and I got into the ditch!

But I have another memory, this time a more pleasant one, of a lovely little cottage, set up high on a hill in Western Pennsylvania, on a vast oil and gas lease where I used to spend most of the summers of my childhood. To reach the lovely little red cottage, which was called Mt. Rebecca, after my sister, we had to climb a great flight of steps that ran all the way up the hill from the foot of it to the cottage. Curving this way and that, with little level places every now and then, the flight of wooden steps mounted right up the hill. Below and above the steps was an earthen path which led to our summer home. And at the top of the path and at the bottom, were great gas torches that burned all night long. The natural gas from the oil wells was piped to each torch, which consisted of nothing but a gas pipe sticking up out of the ground about eight feet into the air with a valve on it to shut off and turn on the gas. And every night at sundown, somebody would turn on the valve and light the torch which made a huge flame leaping up into the air as the gas rushed out of the end of the pipe and burst into a constant flame that lighted up the region round about all night through. How the flames from those two torches lighted up that mountain path! All the way up and down the hill, the light shone, and the path was illuminated from top to bottom. It took a great deal of gas to keep those torches burning all night, but gas was cheap, and they lighted up the path!

Now the Bible is like a light on the pathway of life. There is a text for today that I want to give you, one of the finest texts in the Bible and one which I hope you all will learn. It is in the Book of Psalms, in the 119th Psalm, the 105th verse: "Thy word is a lamp unto my feet, and a light unto my path." God's Word is, of course, the Bible. And our text tells us that the Bible is like a light to our path. Just as a light on a dark night helps us so much on the path in which we are walking, so the Bible will help us in our walk of life.

Is the world all about us in the dark sometimes? Does everything round about us look dark and black? Well, at such a time the Bible will shed light. Just exactly as a flashlight directed upon a sidewalk on a dark night will show us the way, so will the Bible, in the midst of spiritual and mental darkness, shed its gracious light around us.

Is there some ditch that we might fall into along the pathway of life, some spiritual pitfall ahead of us in the darkness of life, some grave danger that we cannot see? The Bible will lighten up the path ahead and will show us the danger spots and the way to go and the way to avoid. Just as a street light would have kept me out of the ditch filled with water that dark night I told you of in the Catskill Mountains, so the Bible will lighten the way of life for us and show us the spiritual and moral dangers and pitfalls that we should avoid.

Is our life like a climb, a high hill to go up, a rocky path over a mountain ahead of us? Often life seems like that, like a climb all the way, like up-hill work, like a rocky and steep ascent, always on and always up. Does life seem like that to us? Well, the Bible will be in our lives a light on the path, to shine across it and along it, to illumine it and make it clear and plain and easy. Like those gas torches shone up and down the pathway up the hillside to that cottage of my childhood, exactly so will the Bible cast its welcome light along the pathway of our lives. " Thy word . . . is a light unto my path."

Why should we walk in darkness, when we can have the light? Remember the Bible will ALWAYS shed light on the pathway of life.

CHAPTER XXXIII

The Mistletoe and the Orchid *

(SUNDAY BEFORE CHRISTMAS)

LUKE 17: 17: " And Jesus answering said, Were there not ten cleansed? but where are the nine? "

OBJECTS: A sprig of mistletoe and an orchid. A piece of artificial mistletoe, the kind used in Christmas decorations, will do if the real article is hard to find; and any undertaker will be glad to lend an artificial orchid from his stock of funeral pieces.

TODAY I have brought with me into the pulpit two specimens from two different kinds of plants. One is a sprig of mistletoe. The other is an orchid. Both the

* The suggestion back of this chapter and much of the botanical information contained in it were given to me by my brother, Lt. Com. A. R. Schofield, U.S.N., and my sister, the late Rebecca F. Schofield, to whom both credit and thanks are due.

mistletoe and the orchid are very wonderful plants. Both of them grow on other plants: shrubs, or bushes or trees. The mistletoe is always found growing on some other living plant, usually some tree. And many kinds of orchids, though not all, are likewise found living on the branches of other living plants, often great trees, too.

You know what the mistletoe is. You always see it at Christmas time used in the homes as part of the holiday decorations. It has thick, green leaves; and short, thick stems; and produces little, white berries. It is very pretty and very much admired. But it is what botanists call a parasite. It lives on another plant or tree. Sometimes it completely covers the other plant it lives on. Sometimes it completely covers a big tree. And it not only lives ON the other. It also lives OFF the other. I mean by that that the other plant or tree feeds it and gives it its living. The mistletoe sends its roots into the tree it lives on and draws its nourishment out of it. It lives off the other. And after a while it draws so much nourishment and food from the plant or tree it lives on, which we call the host, that that tree has none left for itself and it dies. After a while the mistletoe kills the tree it lives on, the tree that feeds it, the tree that gives it its life. For example, you can see great trees that the little mistletoe has killed in the south of our own country; perhaps a mighty water oak, completely covered by the mistletoe plant until the mistletoe has killed it.

Now the orchid is not like the mistletoe. There are many, many different kinds of orchids in the world and most of them are very beautiful. Some of them are very brilliant in color and of a very unusual and peculiar structure. Some of them are very rare indeed. And that makes them very costly to buy. A real, live orchid flower is considered a very wonderful thing to own and a very wonderful gift to give. It is so rare, so beautiful, so costly.

Now many of the orchid plants, not all varieties of course, but many of them, live on other plants or trees, just as the mistletoe does. But the great difference is that while the mistletoe is a parasite, the orchid really is not. It often lives on another plant, or a tree; but it does not get its food from that other plant. It manufactures its own; it doesn't steal it from its host. It only lives on the tree or other plant where it makes its home. It does not steal its food from it nor kill it.

Now do you know that the mistletoe and the orchid make me think of children in the home? And I will tell you why. We live in another's home, do we not, we children? It is not our home we live in, but our parents' home, isn't it? Like the mistletoe and the orchid living on the branches of another plant, on the branches of some great tree perhaps, so children live in the home of another. But which plant are we like, the mistletoe or the orchid? Do we take and never give? Do we act like the mistletoe, taking our food and our very life from other people and never giving anything back in return? Or do we do our part, do we repay something for all the things our parents give to us? Are we like the orchid, which does its part and cares for itself? Do we do our part, do we repay the love and kindnesses our parents shower upon us? They do everything for us. Do we do what we can for them and for ourselves to show them we love them and are thankful to them for all they do for us?

But if children are like the mistletoe and the orchid, so are men in society. Some men get and never give; take and never offer anything in return. Some men live off other men, live off society, as we say, and do nothing to make their own way or to do their own part or to take care of themselves. They are parasites; for they live off other people and do not do their part in the world. But there are other men who contribute what they can to the general welfare; who do their part in the world; who help as well as get help; who give as well as take; who help themselves and do what they can to make the world better. Such men are like orchids; while the men who take and never give are like the mistletoe. Which kind of men and women are we going to be: selfish, greedy parasites; or unselfish, helpful men and women who do their part in the world?

It is exactly so with men and their country. Some people take everything from their country and give nothing back in return, not even thanks. Others do what they can to make their country greater, to show their love for their country, to do their part in making their country the best and the greatest country on the earth. Our country, America, has given us great things: our freedom, the right to make a living, our education and all the blessings and privileges of liberty. Should we not in return do our part to help America that has done so much for us?

One day Jesus healed ten lepers, removing from them that dreadful disease that was so feared and that made them so miserable and that made other people keep away from them. But after He had healed the ten men of their awful disease, only one out of the ten came back to Him to thank Him. "And Jesus answering said, Were there not ten cleansed? but where are the nine?" That is our text this morning, boys and girls. Luke 17: 17: "Where are the nine?" Only one came back to thank the Lord for the wonderful thing He had done for them all. Are we ever like that? Do we receive from God the many and great gifts He is always giving to us and never try to repay Him or to show Him our gratitude? God gives us our life, our health, our very breath, the food we eat, the clothing that covers us, our parents, our homes, our Church, our faith, our salvation. God gives us everything. Are we toward Him like mistletoe, taking but not giving back; receiving but not thanking Him? Or are we like the orchid, doing our part; appreciating what God has done for us and trying to do something for Him in return? Are we like the nine healed lepers who went off and forgot to thank Jesus Christ for their miraculous healing? Or are we like the one who came back to thank Him? Think it over, boys and girls!

CHAPTER XXXIV

What Shall I Give? *

(CHRISTMAS)

❧

MATTHEW 2: 11: "And when they were come into the house, they saw the young child with Mary his mother,

* The story in this chapter is taken from an advertising letter of the magazine, *Time,* and is told here by permission of the publishers.

and fell down, and worshipped him: and when they had opened their treasures, they presented unto him gifts; gold, and frankincense, and myrrh."

OBJECT: A small plush animal of any kind to illustrate the squirrel in the story.

❧

I AM sure that all the boys and girls know that beautiful text in the Bible which tells about the Wise Men bringing their gifts to the Christ Child at the first Christmas that the world ever had. You can find this text in Matthew in the second chapter and at the eleventh verse. " And when they were come into the house, they saw the young child with Mary his mother, and fell down, and worshipped him: and when they had opened their treasures, they presented unto him gifts; gold, and frankincense, and myrrh." They brought gifts to Jesus. We give gifts to each other at Christmas. And each of us asks himself, " What Shall I Give? "

I want to tell you a story that I read the other day. Once upon a time, Mr. Charles M. Schwab, one of the richest men in America, took a little girl to the biggest toy store in this country. He told her to look the store over and to pick out anything she liked and he would buy it for her for Christmas. For three whole hours, the story says, this lucky, little girl and the rich man, the President of Bethlehem Steel Company, one of the biggest and richest companies in the world, searched that whole store from top to bottom for the very best present of all; the one the little girl would like the best and want the most. The manager of the store heard that Mr. Schwab was there to buy a gift and he hurried out to help the rich man and the little girl find something particularly wonderful. Half a dozen clerks and buyers trailed along. They looked very carefully at the $300 doll house with its two baths and running water; they sat in the real train that would carry ten children around the back yard; they played with the talking doll whose wardrobe was worthy of a real princess. At last the little girl said to Mr. Schwab:

" Can I really have anything I want? "

Mr. Schwab smiled, " Yes," and the manager smiled; and all the clerks standing around smiled; and all the buyers who had followed smiled.

" Well, this is what I want," said the little girl; and she picked up a little plush squirrel, marked twenty-five cents; very like this little plush animal I hold in my hand. Anything in that great store could have been hers and she picked a twenty-five-cent toy!

Now I have told you that story because I think it will help us answer our Christmas question, " What shall I give? "

I

It is not the cost of a gift that counts. That little girl did not decide what she wanted by the price mark. And so when we give gifts, it is not the cost that counts. God's Gift to us is the most costly Gift that was ever given—the Gift of His Son, Jesus Christ, our Saviour. And whatever gift we may give can never be anything like that Gift in value or in cost. Our gifts, compared to the Gift that God gave to the world on the first Christmas, are always small and cheap and insignificant. We can never give anything that begins to compare with the great Gift God gave to the world that day. So the cost of a gift is not the thing that counts.

II

But thought should be in every gift, whatever that gift may be. Whatever our gifts and to whomever we give them, let us put thought in them. Let our gifts be thoughtful gifts. Let the gifts we give not be like the one I once heard of when a woman gave her husband a set of new parlor curtains for Christmas. This was not a thoughtful gift, for she wanted those curtains herself and they were really not a gift to her husband at all! But the next year her husband got back at her. For he gave her that year a box of cigars which he wanted for himself and which he used himself. Now neither of these gifts was a thoughtful gift. Both of them were selfish. Our gifts are to be thoughtful gifts. Thought is to be put in our gifts.

III

And love is to be in our gifts. Never forget that. Be sure to put love into every gift you give. It is meaningless unless you do. You might just as well not give your gift, if love is not in it. Give yourself to God. That will be a great gift of love to Him who gave us the greatest Gift of all when He gave us His Son. Give yourself to others. That will also be a great gift of love to those about you, your family and your friends.

"What shall I give?" each of us asks himself. Remember that the cost of the gift is not the thing that counts. Remember that thought must be in your gift. Remember that love must be in it.

140

CHAPTER XXXV

The Worn Out Christmas Tree *
(AFTER CHRISTMAS)

֍

2 TIMOTHY 4: 10: " Demas hath forsaken me."

֍

THERE are many things about Christmas that we all love very much. And one of these is the Christmas tree. It wouldn't be Christmas without the tree, would it? But now Christmas is past and most of us in our homes and in the church and on the streets are taking down our Christmas trees. We carefully take off all the ornaments and streamers and tinsel and lights and pack them all very carefully away to be taken out again and used next year. The needles have been dropping off the branches of the trees like little showers. Shorn of their ornaments and denuded of their needles, the trees look very bare indeed. Then they are taken down and carried out of the houses and thrown away.

What a sad sight a discarded Christmas tree makes! Worn out, thrown away, out on some dump somewhere, no good to anybody any more, how forlorn and sad and dreary it looks. Do you know of anything that looks sadder and more forlorn than a worn out Christmas tree, cast off, thrown away, languishing on a heap of ashes in the back yard? One of the members of our

---

* My sincere thanks go to Mrs. Margaret Webster Backus for permission to quote from her poem, " The Dismantled Christmas Tree," published in her Book, " Poems From My Pen," copyright, 1937, by her.

own church, Mrs. Margaret Webster Backus, has written a poem about just such a sight and because it describes the picture so well I want to read part of it to
you. It is called " The Dismantled Christmas Tree."

" Now isn't it just as sad as can be
    The fate that befalls the Christmas tree?
As pretty a tree as ever was seen,
    Tall and straight and of darkest green,
Trimmed with tinsel and fringe of ice,
    Glittering things and ornaments nice,
Then strung with many a colored light
    To make it a blaze of glory by night. . . .

" When no one was left with a song or story
    The proud little tree was shorn of its glory.
And the tree that had made them all so glad
    Was thrown outside in a world cold and sad,
Where 'twas tossed about and jeered at by boys
    For whom it had given its load of toys.
'Twas set in a snow-bank, hit with snowballs hard,
    Then thrown on the rubbish heap out in the yard.

" Now isn't it sad, when it has been such a friend,
    That a Christmas tree should come to that end? . . ."

How true her poem is! And it is true not only of a
Christmas tree that we use and then throw away. It is
true of other things, as well. For very often we use
something and then throw it away. Maybe it is a toy
with which we have played and now we are tired of it.
Maybe it is a doll that has been broken and we throw
away. Maybe it is a book we no longer want. We use
these things, wear them out or break them, get tired of
them and throw them away. And how often the thing
we throw away presents a very sorry sight!

But in just the same way sometimes we cast off our friends. After we have used them, after we have gotten all we can out of them, we tire of them and are done with them and we cast them off; we throw them away. It is a sad thing and a dreary thing that this happens, but it sometimes does. There is a text in the Bible which describes this very thing. It is in Paul's second letter to Timothy, the 4th chapter and the 10th verse, and it says, "Demas hath forsaken me." Paul is writing to his friend Timothy and he says here that another friend, Demas, has left him, gone away from him, thrown him off, deserted him. His friend, Demas, tired of Paul and thinking he could get nothing further out of him, having used him all he could, deserted him, cast him off. I do not know anything sadder than that, for a friend to throw away a friend!

And so I want to say to you this morning, don't throw away the real value of Christmas when you throw away the tree. When the tree is worn out, you have to dispose of it, of course. But don't throw away the real meaning of Christmas with the tree. For Christmas means joy and kindness and Christ Himself. Be sure that you keep these things! Be sure that the Christmas joy remains with you all through the year. Be sure that the Christmas kindness stays right at your side. Don't throw away your love for each other that is created at Christmas. And most of all don't throw away Christ Himself. For He is the real meaning of Christmas, after all. Keep Him whatever you do. Be most careful not to throw Christ away with the Christmas tree.

And also, let me say to you, don't throw away the true values of your friends. Don't cast off your friends as you do a broken toy or a useless book or a worn-out Christmas tree. Be loyal and true to your friends. Keep them and cherish them. Don't throw them away, for they have meant much to you in the past and will mean more to you in the future.